THE SPANISH CIVIL WAR
The Road to Madrid

THE DIARY OF DONALD GALLIE
MEMBER OF THE SCOTTISH MEDICAL AID UNIT
THE SPANISH CIVIL WAR SEPTEMBER–DECEMBER 1936

Transcribed and edited by Donald Gallie's daughter, Nina Stevens
Photograph below by Michael Gallie

Donald Gallie 1911–1999

Map of the route the ambulance unit took to Madrid, and the return sea journey to Marseille from Alicante

Sea-front Esplanade Alicante 1936

ACKNOWLEDGEMENTS: I would like to thank Linda Palfreeman for writing the Introduction, Richard Baxell and Jim Jump for their encouragement and support, and Denis Havard for coordinating the book design.

Family and friends mentioned in Donald Gallie's Diary
Donald's parents, Charles and Margaret Gallie
Roy, Donald's brother and his girlfriend, Edna Kenley
Betty, Donald's sister
Karin, Donald's girlfriend in Sweden
Cousins in Belfast, Emma, Alex and Aileen
Uncle George, his mother's brother
Family friends Mrs. Oswald and Mr. and Mrs. Robert Holley

Front cover: The Russian planes arrive in Madrid on November 6th 1936
Page 64: La Pasionara statue for the freedom of Spain sculpted by Artur Dooley stands on
Custom House Quay, Glasgow. (photograph by Nina Stevens)
All photos (except eight) were taken by Donald Gallie

2 4 6 8 10 9 7 5 3 1

First published 2019 in Great Britain by
SUSSEX ACADEMIC PRESS
PO Box 139
Eastbourne BN24 9BP

Distributed in North America by
SUSSEX ACADEMIC PRESS
Independent Publishers Group
814 N. Franklin Street
Chicago, IL 60610

British Library Cataloguing in Publication Data
A CIP catalogue record for this book is available from the British Library.

Library of Congress Cataloging-in-Publication Data
To be applied for.

Printed by TJ International, Padstow, Cornwall.

Contents

Introduction

When a failed right wing military coup provoked civil war in Spain, in July 1936, the Spanish government made a worldwide plea for help. The British government (like the governments of other countries such as France and the United States) declared a policy of 'non-intervention'. Nevertheless, ordinary citizens of these countries responded en masse. In Britain, Aid Spanish Committees sprang up in every major town and city, nationwide. Film shows, fêtes, rallies and fairs, book clubs and cake sales were among the great variety of events held in towns and villages throughout the country, in order to raise funds to send aid to Spain. They were used with the dual aim of both raising money for Spain and of highlighting the Republican cause. The National joint committee for Spanish Relief (NJCSR) was set up to coordinate these many and varied fundraising enterprises.

In Scotland there was a tremendous support for the Spanish Republic, even in areas wracked by poverty and unemployment. By mid-1937, Glasgow alone had 15 NJCSR groups.[1] Initial fundraising endeavours were spontaneous and ad hoc, but these were gradually succeeded by more organized campaigns of a collective nature. The 'Foodship for Spain' campaign represented an exceptional example of inter-city co-operation in Scotland, with £10,000 being raised to send out a cargo of foodstuffs and medical supplies to the Republic. On 18 December 1936, 1,000 tons of emergency provisions were shipped out to Spain from Broomielaw Quay, Glasgow arriving in Spain in time for Christmas.[2]

Nowhere was empathy more keenly felt for the working people of Spain than among the people of Glasgow, which became the hub of the Scottish Aid for Spain movement. At the city's May Day celebrations in 1937, 15,000 people turned out to demonstrate their solidarity with the Spanish Republic. Gray (2009) describes the fervor aroused by the conflict:

> Political meetings on the subject of Spain became commonplace in Glasgow. As a happy side-effect they acted as fundraisers, with buckets passed around for donations. In terms of attendance, the meetings were an overwhelming success; it seemed Glaswegians had become as fanatical about the Spanish Republic as they were about Celtic and Rangers.[3]

An Aid Spain shop was established at 11 Union Street, Glasgow, as a collection centre for food, milk and medical supplies as well as for monetary donations. Businesses contributed food and other goods for Spain and factory workers gave their free time to prepare and pack consignments whilst garages repaired and reconditioned vehicles for use as ambulances and other evacuation transport. Glasgow was also home to an enterprise which was to make a significant contribution to the Spanish Republic—the Scottish Ambulance Unit.

The Scottish Ambulance Unit was the brainchild of a wealthy Glaswegian philanthropist Sir Daniel Macaulay Stevenson (1851–1944). Stevenson became involved in civic affairs in the

---

1. A unified Scottish Joint Committee for Spanish Relief would eventually be established in February 1938.

2. The trades councils proposed sending a second ship, though this never actually materialized, due to the intensification of the blockade on Spanish waters.

3. Daniel Gray, *Homage to Caledonia: Scotland and the Spanish Civil War* (Edinburgh: Luath Press Paperback edition, 2009), p. 109.

1890s, being elected to Glasgow's City Council in 1892. He later served as City Treasurer and then as Lord Provost, from 1911 to 1914, when he received a baronetcy. Stevenson was responsible for a number of socially progressive measures in the city, including making cultural facilities more accessible to working class Glaswegians.

After his retirement from politics, Stevenson continued to lend his support to worthy causes—especially that of furthering international understanding among young people—a project which he pursued as Chancellor of the University of Glasgow.[4] Sir Daniel's exceptional merits and his extreme generosity were publicly acknowledged in those countries to which he had extended his schemes for fostering international understanding and in France, Germany, Italy and Spain and his name was familiar to the international press.[5]

In early September 1936, Sir Daniel Macaulay Stevenson created a committee of well-known Scottish academics and aristocracy to provide backing for his plan to send out a medical unit to the Spanish Republic. As well as relying on public donations, funding for the SAU came in no small part from Sir Daniel himself, his wealthy friends and from the Trades Union Congress (TUC).[6] In his role of the General Secretary of the TUC, Sir Walter Citrine was to play a very significant role in the funding of humanitarian aid to Spain, and over the coming years he would give constant support to Sir Daniel Stevenson and the Scottish Ambulance Unit. Citrine also pointed out that in order to maximize public support for such an endeavor, the humanitarian, non-political nature of its work should be emphasized.[7]

Eventually the Scottish Ambulance Unit was ready to depart. It comprised six ambulances and a supply truck carrying stores and medical equipment, together with a team of twenty volunteers (19 men and one woman). There was one doctor, Louis Levin as well as drivers, mechanics, first-aiders and other helpers. John Boyd and Fred McMahon were from Belfast and the rest were from Glasgow and the west of Scotland: Robert Budge, George Burleigh, William Cox, George Crawford, William Freebairn (son of ex-Provost Freebairn), Harry Girvan, Duncan Johnstone, Angus McClean, Alex McLennan, Duncan Newbigging, Walter Perfect, Ernst Porter, Herbert Richmond, Thomas Watters and Donald Gallie. The only woman in the team was the Unit's commandant, Fernanda Jacobsen.

Not long after its arrival in Spain, the Unit was pitched into active duty. It set up headquarters in Aranjuez, some fifty kilometers south of Madrid from where it served on the Toledo front to the south-west of the capital. During the early days of the conflict the Unit's help proved invaluable to the *Sanidad Militar*, still in a state of relative disorganization and stretched to its limits due to heavy casualties. During fierce fighting, and in great personal danger to themselves, the Scottish volunteers rescued fallen Republican troops at Olias del Rey, Illescas and Cabañas de

————————————

4. Stevenson was Chancellor of the University of Glasgow from 1934– 1944, in addition to funding various enterprises in Glasgow, Sir Daniel made generous endowments to other universities both at home and abroad including, for example, a gift of £10,000 to the British Institute in Florence and the endowment of a Chair in International History at the University of London (*Daily Record and Mail 19*, Friday 18 January 1935). (IBA Archives, Marx Memorial Library, London).

5. In the year before the military uprising that would lead to the Spanish Civil War, the Spanish newspapers carried features on Sir Daniel's student exchange schemes. *La Vanguarida* newspaper, for instance, reports on the visit to Spain of Miss Fernanda Jacobsen, Sir Daniel's secretary and a member of the Executive Committee for the Concession of Grants and Student Exchanges. 'Sir Daniel' is described as 'a great enthusiast of the culture and history of Spain who endeavours to strengthen the cultural relationship between Spain and Scotland.' (*La Vanguardia*, Sunday 22 September 1935).

6. This is partly to do with the fact that fundraising appeals were largely restricted to within Scotland.

7. These words would later prove very significant, in the light of the internal struggles of the SAU, caused by misinterpretation of its general aims.

la Segra, administering first aid and ferrying the wounded to hospitals in Madrid. From here onwards, the Authorities would call upon the services of the SAU whenever there was an action resulting in (or likely to result in) significant numbers of casualties.

The team's valiant and tireless work soon earned it an excellent reputation among Republican forces and as news of its remarkable work spread, volunteers became affectionately known as *Los Brujos*—The Wizards.

However, the off-duty activities of some of the SAU's members were earning it an altogether different kind of reputation, and the Unit was soon to become immersed in the first of the scandals that were to tarnish its good name and jeopardize its future.[8] Donald Gallie was a member of the first SAU team to arrive in Madrid (there would be three successive expeditions).

Donald Gallie was 24 years of age when Civil War broke out in Spain. A keen sportsman, Donald played rugby for his home town Lenzie, where he lived with his parents, Charles and Margaret, his brother Roy and his sister Betty. The Gallies shared a strong sense of commitment, and this, together with Donald's love of travel and adventure, is what impelled him to volunteer for service in Spain with the Scottish Ambulance Unit, where his skills as mechanic would prove invaluable. What follows are Donald's diary entries for the time he spent in Spain with the Unit— September to December 1936.

---

8. For further details of the SAU's activities in Spain, see Linda Palfreeman, *Aristocrats, Adventurers and Ambulances: British Medical Units in the Spanish Civil War.* (Eastbourne: Sussex Academic Press / the Canada Blanch Centre for Spanish Studies, 2014)

Donald's snapshot of Barcelona 27th September 1936

Map

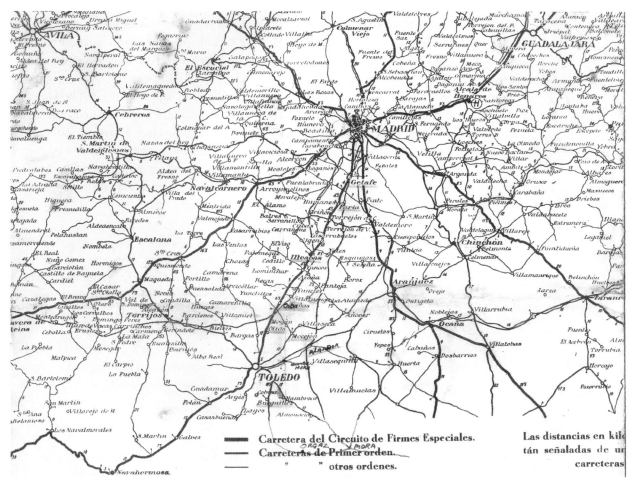

Map showing the key positions of the Ambulance men in between Madrid and Toledo September–December 1936

September 1936

THURSDAY 17TH SEPTEMBER

I said goodbye to the folks at home this morning and left as a member of the Scottish Medical Aid Unit en route for Spain. My departure was an unhappy business, especially for little Mother who is bound to feel the parting very acutely, and for Grandpa who doesn't expect to be alive when I return.

Karin, my girlfriend, sent me a farewell letter and so did my cousin, Aileen. The Unit consists of nineteen men, one woman interpreter, six ambulances and a truck. The convoy left Sir Daniel Stevenson's house and went to George Square in Glasgow. Here I met my sister, Betty, Dad and Mr. Oswald, a family friend, for a final goodbye and soon we were bound for Abington. We stopped here for tea at a large farm belonging to Duncan Newbigging's father. (Duncan is a member of our team). By night time we were in Appleby and we were to stay for the night. The vans were run into a field, then we had some supper and so to bed.

FRIDAY 18TH SEPTEMBER

After a good night's rest we rose early and were on the road by 9 a.m. We made good progress and stopped at Boroughbridge for lunch and then on to Doncaster. Along the route we have been stopping frequently for no apparent reason. The men seem to be O.K. but rough and ready. We have not been getting regular meal hours. George Burleigh from Kilsyth and Hal Girvan and I had a fish and chips tea. We have been given 3d each for a cup of tea.

Finally we stopped for the night at a place called Longbennington at 8.30 p.m. We got to bed immediately after our supper. It is to be noted that officially we have had nothing to eat except a cup of tea since 2.30 p.m. There is a lack of organization there somewhere or else a lack of decency to the men.

SATURDAY 19TH SEPTEMBER

We were up very early—about 5 a.m. and were on the road by 6 a.m. It was very cold and a mist shrouded the land. Nevertheless we went merrily on till we came to Royston where we had breakfast—a right good one. An hour later we were on the road again. It was fine going along the Great North Road. About 1 o'clock we struck London, but didn't stop there at all. On we went till we hit Canterbury at 4 p.m. Here again let it be noticed that we had nothing to eat from 9.30 a.m. till 4.30 p.m. At Canterbury some of us had a stroll through the Cathedral. It was simply wonderful, so dignified and awe inspiring. We had a stroll around some of the old fashioned streets too, and I wrote a postcard or two—one to Mother and one to Karin.

At 7 o'clock we were on the road again and after passing through undulating terrain we arrived an hour later in Dover. We had covered 195 miles. The vans were stored in the harbour shed and we had the luxury of sleeping in the Grand Hotel. It was great to be bedded down in a comfortable bed again.

SUNDAY 20TH SEPTEMBER

I awoke at 7 a.m. and after washing and shaving, went downstairs for breakfast. As soon as this was over we went to the sheds and loaded the vans with more goods—phew! it was a hectic half hour. Oh! I forgot—last night on arriving at Dover I received a letter and my wrist watch from Mother. Her letter showed plainly that she is missing me. I pray that God will give her strength, courage and happiness.

Well, to continue with the day's log. By 11.30 a.m. all the vans were loaded onto the little ferry and off we set. It was a glorious sail. Cloudless sky, a stiff breeze and a good heave. Some were sick but Oh Boy! it was good. The crossing was accomplished in one and a half hours and I set foot on French soil for the first time. The lorries were unloaded and in another hour we had passed through the customs. We drove to a square and parked there. Just opposite the parking place dinner had been ordered in a cafe and there we partook of our first meal. Really the only strange thing was the wine.

After dinner we drove through the town and made a detour by Boulogne. It was unusual driving along the road lined with trees but with no hedges—no hedges to be seen anywhere. On each side of the road lay cultivated fields but no cattle. We drove for about 30-40 miles and finished at a little place called Neauville. Here the mayor of the village, who was a wealthy farmer, allowed us to park the buses in his yard and we slept very comfortably in his hay loft.

MONDAY 21ST SEPTEMBER

We arose early this morning and before we set off there was a dirty piece of work done. We could see, since leaving Glasgow that there has been considerable friction among the officers. The head is an American-Jew doctor, Levin, and he is "peculiar". He informed us that Miss Jacobsen as Liaison Officer had no right to give orders and was to be disobeyed. She has not given any orders. It was a lousy speech calling her down before the men.

We moved off with this rankling in our minds and about 11 o'clock we stopped and Boyd, the Transport Officer, refused to proceed on as Doctor Levin was issuing and countermanding orders.

The men gave Levin their opinion and suggested his resignation—he is genuine but he is not a leader. At lunch he said he would consider it. We stopped at Chartres for the night in the school. Next day we moved on to Limoges where there was more trouble. He accused Miss Jacobsen of wanting to go to Madrid for ulterior motives—to rescue a friend. The men are extremely discontented with all this and the indifferent way of having food from the cook. We telegraphed the news to Glasgow and asked for instructions.

Wednesday morning a wire came to say, "Proceed Madrid, pay Levin's expenses home and put Duncan Newbigging in charge". We stopped here all day and repacked our vans. We were billeted in a small hall belonging to the Union Philanthropique de Beaublanc.

On we went and by Thursday night we were in Toulouse. Here we were billeted in a big hall—Foyer du Peuple and we slept on the stage.

At Limoges many of the men went on a spree in the early hours and I had to rush about the town trying to find them and collect them with another man. Finally we found them in a whore shop—we went in for them and we got some home.

However to proceed. From Toulouse we went to Perpignan and drove all day through fields of vines loaded with black grapes. At Perpignan it was extremely hot. We had a slap up feed at the Hotel de France and I collected a letter from Mum and one from Dad saying all was O.K. at home. I wrote letters to Mum, Karin, Aileen and post cards to my brother Roy and Grandma.

We passed through customs at 7 p.m. and so were in Spain. It was dark when we entered Spain by the twisted mountain road and as we passed the villages I could see that the people were happy to see us—especially the women folk.

Once or twice along the road we had to stop for sandbag obstructions. Then I discovered that Spanish time is one hour behind French time so we arrived at the town of Figueras by 7.30 p.m. We were made very welcome and an excellent hotel placed at our disposal. Here we had a well cooked feed that we haven't had since we left. Soup, potatoes and beans, fish, succulent meat and chips, egg custard, grapes and apples, all accompanied with plenty of wine and soda water.

After this we were met by the President of the local Red Cross. He appeared to be a brilliant little man who spoke good English and got his science degree in Glasgow. He showed us over the town—the new hospital he is building from a commandeered house—workers clubs—everywhere we went we were welcomed with open arms. Spain has certainly made a great impression on my mind. I got to bed by midnight dead tired.

SATURDAY 26TH SEPTEMBER

After an excellent sleep I rose about 6 a.m. and did a bit of writing. We had breakfast at 7.15 a.m. and this consisted of large cups of very white coffee (i.e. 90% milk) and sweet biscuits. It was very nice but to us hardly satisfying.

At 8 a.m. we went up to the hilltop house where our buses were parked for the night. It was simply magnificent looking across the clear countryside to the jagged Pyrenees, purple in the morning haze rearing their peaks into the blue sky. The engines were seen to and soon we were on the road again. The convoy being headed by an official car flying the government flag. Passing through the various towns and villages, the only indications of warfare are the sandbag obstructions as we enter the town and leave—also the militia hanging about.

The drive along the shores of the Mediterranean was marvelous. We wound in and out, up and down. The cliffs come very close to the shore. Sometimes the views were breathtaking and just typical of the views I have seen in pictures. The sun shone down on a baked land and the heat was terrific. We arrived in Barcelona about 2 p.m. and expected a civic reception but this was not forthcoming. We wandered about the place feeling absolutely starved while our escort went here and there arranging things. It was 4 p.m. before we touched a morsel of food—9 hours without any food. We were supposed to go for a bathe in the sea after this but it was not possible. Instead we went to an hotel and stood by while refugees in hundreds flocked in and out. It was pathetic. Many of the women crying and all their worldly belongings beside them.

We were taken to another hotel and got to our rooms. At 8 o'clock we had our supper and by 10 p.m. I was in bed.

While at supper a Glasgow lad joined us—he had joined up with the militia. He told us of some of the horrors and heroism of the Spanish workers. At the beginning of the revolution the troops entrenched behind machine guns were killed by men with no other weapons than sticks and stones. These men lined up behind each other and charged. The front of the charge was mown down but the others charged on and on. The first men acted as shields for the men behind and when they went down the second row acted as shields. When the last arrived at the guns they jumped over and battered the gunners to death with bricks and clubs. Then a little later when both sides had guns—all people in the streets were mown down from roof tops. The streets were littered with dead and dying. The bugle would be blown—both sides stopped firing—ambulances rushed in, cleared the streets, rushed back and the firing went on. Then the bugle would blow again, etc.

SUNDAY 27TH SEPTEMBER

I rose at 6.30 am, washed, shaved, went down for breakfast and had it—cup of coffee and two rolls.

It doesn't feel like Sunday. We waited a while till the buses were filled, etc. and then a car took us up to the parking place. With the car in front as a guide we set off merrily. We were accompanied out of town and then we parted company as the road was perfectly clear for Valencia. It was simply breathtaking watching the magnificent buildings of Barcelona receding in the morning sunlight.

I wrote a letter to Mum and gave it to an English chap to post. On we went merrily with me sitting in the back of No.7. I had sort of dozed off when we stopped and was thinking it one of our frequent stops when I heard a shout of "Help, boys, Help!" Round I rushed and what a sight met my gaze. No 4 wagon had fallen over on its' side at a nasty bend. I sprinted up but found the driver and his passenger safe. We unloaded it of all its petrol tins and then the goods, and in less than no time it was empty.

I took a few snaps of the tumble while the others were fussing about. Then ropes and shackles were brought and tied to the chassis—discussions as to how to raise it went full force and meanwhile some of the chaps and a few natives got under the top side and lifted her up. Examination showed little damage and soon we were on the road again.

Capsized No. 4 ambulance on the road from Barcelona to Valencia

We stopped at Tarragona about 3 o'clock to feed. Here we had a good meal of ever so many courses including the national Spanish dish. This is a dish with a mixture of rice, mussels, eels, snails and steak. Many of the men wouldn't touch it but I found it very nice tasting and did full justice to it. Next we took the cars to the garage and judge our surprise when it proved to be the local bullring!!

While various discussions were taking place we got out the football and had a game of "Keep-ie Up". Some of the Spaniards are very quick on their feet. We were quite a while in the bullring and many of us just itching to get down to the beach for a bathe.

Finally we commandeered a car and set off. We stripped and plunged into the Mediterranean—yours truly was first in. Oh Boy! It was almost lukewarm and absolutely glorious! The sun had set and we disported ourselves in the moonlight. One of the locals gave us a little drink of aniseed liqueur and it felt fine.

We returned to our hotel. A court martial was held on the driver who had driven the car which had capsized and we found that it was an accident but Perfect, the driver, was inclined to recklessness.

We had supper and I was in bed by 9.30 or 10 p.m. Many of the other others went out for a walk and to search for the nearest brothel. I slept soundly till 6.30 a.m.

MONDAY 28TH SEPTEMBER

We had breakfast—coffee and rolls and set off about 10 a.m. for Valencia. Really nothing of interest happened until we reached Vinaroz. Here we had lunch about 2 p.m. What a lunch—we had actually to refuse food. We started off with soup, then potatoes and beans, next came fish, then the national dish, followed by beef cutlets and finally a jelly—lemonade and wine as much as could be consumed.

Feeling very full and sleepy I changed places in the front and went behind to sleep. It was fine. I woke just as it was getting dark—there is no twilight here. We went in to Castellon about 7.30 p.m. and got filled up with petrol. We were escorted through crowds of people to the Comte de Guerre and there we had whisky and soda, some lemonade and all had biscuits. We got a cheer, a clap and a send off, and we were bucked up by it. A long journey followed and we were glad to arrive at Valencia by 10.45 p.m. Here there was a big delay as the people of Castellon had not been able to get through to Valencia.

About 11.45 p.m. we had a meal of sausages and bread. I had lemonade and iced lemon crush. We started a sing song and it was funny reflecting that here we were at 1 a.m. singing away in the basement room of a cafe in Valencia after being on the road since 6.30 a.m. The cars were parked in a garage and we were parked in the Regina Hotel. I tumbled into bed about 2 a.m. after thanking the Master for all His blessings.

TUESDAY 29TH SEPTEMBER

Aileen is 21 years old today and I cannot let her know that I wish her many happy returns. Before breakfast I started to write her a letter and then it was interrupted, however I completed it before going to bed.

It was decided amongst the drivers that we must have a rest for a day in Valencia. We made out that it would be highly dangerous for the cars to proceed and this was fairly accurate. Consequently I rushed around the town in a car seeing various committees for the necessary chits for oil, gear oil and distilled water. At 1 o'clock we had lunch and spent all afternoon clearing out the sump and gear boxes and putting in fresh oil. We tightened up chassis bolts and brakes and hosed down the body work. It was grand. At 8.30 p.m. we had supper and because it was not up to the usual standard some men were complaining—yet it was a perfectly good meal.

WEDNESDAY 30TH SEPTEMBER

We were up early this morning and as the Hotel Alhambra staff weren't up we took ourselves off to an adjacent cafe and had breakfast—a good breakfast. Two glasses of white coffee, a boiled egg and two rolls. About 10 a.m. we were on the road with our accompanying car leading the way. We stopped at a small place called Tarancón at 8 p.m. The road to Tarancón was not very interesting as it passed through veritable desert land. Dry sandy brown waste for miles and miles. Sometimes we struck valleys and here was to be found villages with the peasants out tilling their scanty fields. We always knew when we were approaching one of these villages for along the road we passed sleepy eyed mules and donkeys pulling their carts with the dogs chained to them.

One part of the road was extremely interesting and here we crossed a big canyon. The road twisted and turned right down to the bottom and then crossed the river and turned and twisted up to the top. It was truly awe-inspiring.

We arrived at Tarancón and had to appear on the balcony of the local town hall and acknowledge the cheers of the crowd. I got digs in a hotel (converted farmhouse).

Beach and mountain view

October 1936

THURSDAY 1ST OCTOBER

We were up this morning by 9.30 a.m. There was no indication of warfare and soon we reached Madrid which appeared as a large city with high beautiful buildings set in an arid country. We journeyed round the town and shook hands with the Foreign Minister in the Government buildings. Next we went to the garage and then to the Hotel Nacional (see photo below). Here in this magnificent and luxurious hotel George and I got a splendid room with all conveniences including a bathroom and toilet.

We washed and went down to the basement where the grill room is and there had a first class meal. Soon after dinner I wrote a note to Mother and then got to bed.

HOTEL NACIONAL - MADRID

FRIDAY 2ND OCTOBER

I was up about 7 a.m. and had breakfast. The whole day was spent in the garage. We emptied our vans and filled them again. The vans were taken to be greased and filled with petrol. I got to bed early but was wakened during the night by rifle fire and the faint sound of bombs exploding. There was heavy knocking at several doors but none came to ours so I fell asleep again.

SATURDAY 3RD OCTOBER

We were downstairs by 7.15 a.m. this morning as per orders but it was 8.30 a.m. before we had breakfast. I was told that there was a bombing raid and all those of the top floor were told to go down to the bottom floor and several soldiers were sniping at possible spies.

Well, after breakfast we went down for the buses and left about 10 a.m. One and a half hours later we arrived at Aranjuez where we intend to have our base hospital.

We emptied the cans and were asked to go out on an emergency. No. 7 left for Burguillos with three stretchers. We arrived there over horrible roads. We did nothing but managed to bring a wounded man home. He had been shot through the shoulder and the bullet had landed in his thumb. We gave him some morphia tablets. We arrived home at 9.30 and delivered him to the hospital. I got to bed at 11 p.m.

Hal writing at the Hotel Nacional

SUNDAY 4TH OCTOBER

I was up at 4 a.m. and by 5.30 a.m. No 7 was on the road. We followed our guide and he took us over a terrible road to the important station of Algador. Here we were left and had to wait from 8 a.m. to 10 a.m. while our guide went to the front line. From our station we could see the Alcazar of Toledo and the town itself. There were hundreds of soldiers—Oh! What a mob. All were peasants, dirty, unkempt, unshaven and smelly. The place was very dirty but later it was cleaned up. We got four stretcher cases and conveyed them to our base. But Oh! What dust! Clouds and clouds rolled in behind us and we were quite white when we arrived. Next we went to our house which is a beautiful banker's residence, had a wash and some dinner. At 2.30 p.m. our guide who is a captain and medical officer guided us back to Algador in his little car. At Algador he informed us that he was going to take us near the lines. (Algador is about 6 miles from Toledo). On we went for 4 miles. Here we stopped at a farm house where an ambulance had been hidden and camouflaged.

A few minutes later we went on (George Burleigh, Fred McMahon and I) in our No. 7, the little car leading us. About three-quarters of a mile from Toledo the road curved and we started to hear "Whiez, Whiez, Whiez," and all round us little puffs of dirt appeared on the road.

Next we noticed our guides car reversing and thought that he was going to take cover down a little cart track. But no. He reversed right up to us and signaled to us to reverse as well. Still the rifle bullets "wheezed" past us. It was eerie to say the least.

Our guide dodged behind us and then George and I decided to leave No 7 and run for shelter. This we did and shouted to Fred to scram too. We ran along the side of the shallow cutting and dodged behind some bushes.

Suddenly we heard a cannon roar, then a long whine.

Down flat on our faces.

BANG!! and the earth shook. The shell had landed about 20 ft from No. 7.

"Wheeng, wheeng" went the bullets and we jogged along for 20 ft and down.

R-R-ROAR up above two monoplanes circled about 1,500-2,000 ft. They passed over and we fell flat again.

BOOM!! The earth and air shivered. BOOM!! Up we got and ran for 20 yds.

BANG! BANG! went the shells some near us and most just missing No.7. We retreated still further and above appeared three more planes.

Down flat again. BOOM!! BOOM!!

"Another bomb to come", says I, but none came.

"What about a fag?", says Fred.

"O.K." said George.

"Have you any objections to me relieving the pressure?" said I.

"Not at all, don't mind us"

BANG!! BANG!! BANG!!

"Come on lads a little further back". My mouth was as dry as a lime kiln. Not a drop of saliva would come.

We retreated still further and left the road, taking cover under some olive trees. Still they pounded No 7 and every few minutes we fell on our faces flat on the ground with the sweat streaming down our faces we bid goodbye to No.7. I suggested another spurt and George says "Ach! Let the sweat clog on ye!"

Finally we reached the farm dressing station, pausing to pick up a piece of shrapnel and high explosive which had landed beyond us.

We waited there till twilight and walked back. We reached No. 7 in darkness and, lo and behold, it still existed. Not a sound was heard. But what is that? A pool of water under the radiator. We tied our kerchiefs round the rear lamp to prevent the brake light showing but it was of no use so we removed the bulb. No. 7 was reversed and we crawled away along the dark road stopping at the dressing station and Algador. We arrived at Aranjuez at 10 p.m. having filled up the radiator umpteen times. We found a bullet hole right through the middle of the radiator.

We got to bed at about 11.30 p.m. and I took two sleeping tablets.

MONDAY 5TH OCTOBER

I had a sound, dreamless sleep last night and awoke very much refreshed. After breakfast Fred, George and I cleaned our No. 7 thoroughly. This took us quite a time as the dust was thick everywhere.

After lunch I fell asleep. While I was sleeping No 7 was called to the hospital to convey a patient to Madrid. The patient was none other than our captain-doctor of yesterday who had half his face torn away. Officially it was in a road accident, but he told our C.O. that it was shrapnel. He was given two days to live.

Bedtime came as usual and that was that.

TUESDAY 6TH OCTOBER

Yours truly is 25 years old today. It was fine thinking that at home Mum, Dad and Betty would be saying it was my birthday and also Karin in Stockholm and maybe Aileen in Belfast. I really did nothing today but eat, sleep and write to Mum and Karin.

WEDNESDAY 7TH OCTOBER

All that happened today was that the inaction going amongst those of us not out on duty. There were heated quarrels about food, etc. which when boiled down, came to nothing.

THURSDAY 8TH OCTOBER

This forenoon George, Fred and I were glad to receive orders to proceed to Burguillos in the afternoon. About 4.30 p.m. we got underway having been delayed by conveying two patients from the hospital to the station. On we went over the rocky road to Mora. At Mora we lost our way and took the wrong turning so in about twenty minutes we found ourselves among vineyards. On we went in the approaching darkness and realized we were lost, with no compass.

At a meeting of ways or rather tracks, we decided on the left hand track. After dodging rocks and mighty boulders we saw lights ahead and landed at Orgaz. By 7 p.m. we arrived at Burguillos. A ration of biscuits and chocolate followed, and out came the sleeping bags.

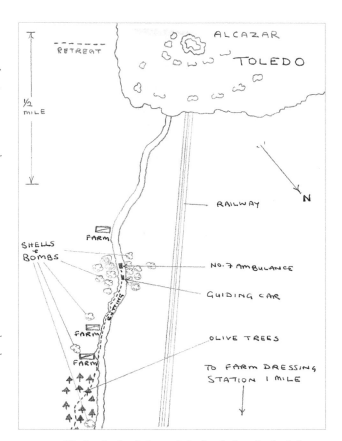

Donald's sketch of ambulances being bombed south of Toledo

George, left, and Donald with No. 7 ambulance. The teddy bear mascot hides the bullet hole in the radiator.

FRIDAY 9TH OCTOBER

I had a restless night with the hard boards under me and the thought that as we had run No. 7 into a farm courtyard, it was an awkward place for sudden evacuation. However I did sleep and rose at 7.30 a.m. in the chilly morning air. There was a blue cloudless sky above with the rising sun in the east.

Occasionally came the boom of artillery but otherwise all was quiet. The farm house which is a big one was full of troops and oh! what smells and what a mess! It is hardly possible to describe it. Papers, tin cans, feathers from plucked fowls, occasionally the innards of a sheep which had been killed for meat—phew! Horrible flies in their millions. We went up to the clearing station in the village and received five cases of sickness. One had an ulcer in the stomach, two had lung trouble and two had V.D. Off we set and arrived at Mora at midday.

I received a present of a small Spanish-English dictionary, and was lent a large scale map by a very nice "Medico". George decided to go "home" for a good lunch and to get everything disinfected. So off we set, promising to return for the Medico at 4 p.m.

About half way to Aranjuez we were stopped and handed a note written by our C.O. to us. The note instructed us to proceed immediately to Aranjuiez, leave the car and all medical stores behind, taking only our personal kit. On we went flabbergasted. Conjectures, surmises, explanations, opinions were discussed galore.

By 1 p.m. we were in Aranjuez and there were informed that all our medical stores, etc. were commandeered by the Government and we were to proceed to Madrid with our personal belongings. Of course it was pure bedlam and we thought that we would be back in Scotland in a few days. However, before we left, two cases were broken open and dispersed among the members—or at least among some members—in other words, looted. A case of whisky and a case containing maybe 1,000 cigarettes. Our C.O. discovered the loss and made an inquiry. Some of the chaps owned up to taking the fags—George Burleigh, Fred McMahon and Steve Richmond. The others denied it and to my knowledge—Malcolm, Perfect and Fairbairn had taken a good supply of fags. There was a shindig and no one admitted taking the whisky. Just before we left Perfect came in drunk "Nuff sed."

A bus came for us and landed us in Madrid. At Madrid Perfect tried to pick a fight with Duncan Newbigging. All the while plans were discussed and rejected and by bedtime we had learnt that our papers were not quite in order and each of us was to be given a permit.

SATURDAY 10TH OCTOBER

As usual George and I had the same room and so we appeared downstairs for breakfast together. Any further news? We were under arrest? There was very little we did not think of. I personally thought that some of the men who were operating on the Olias and Cabañas front in their drunkenness had caused a bad scene and the military commandant had just commandeered their buses. I was told that Jack Boyd, our transport officer, had, in a drunken state, issued highly traitorous statements.

However the news came through that no orders had been issued from Madrid for the commandeering of our ambulances and profuse apologies followed from the War Minister. It had been purely an unauthorized local commandant's orders.

Now George Crawford and Ernest Porter wanted to go home as they had had enough. Porter, however, was absolutely determined. It had gone to his brain and with some drink in him he had an obsession to start a unit of his own. Our C.O. wanted George and I to look after him till it was train time at 11p.m.

In two hours we strove with him in his bedroom trying to pass the time. It was hard work. He wanted to leave immediately and take us with him. We wanted to "think it over". Plans and more plans were discussed and finally by 8 p.m. we had persuaded him to go downstairs for supper and assured him of our support.

To return a little. At supper there was a disgraceful scene. McClean was drunk and in a fighting mood. The table was in an uproar—he wanted to fight various people. Some of the others were drunk too and many of us were so disgusted that we left as soon as possible. Of course the Swedish woman and German woman were there too. We met these two women when we came to Madrid and McClean, Perfect and McLennan and one or two others "made friends" with them. Soon they were taking their meals with us. Then they met these men at Olias and there were disgraceful happenings there—drunkenness and immorality. In fact it is asserted by several witnesses that Jack Boyd and Perfect, when drunk, were shouting about taking no f.....ing orders from a communistic government and going over to the rebels. All of this is the presence of English speaking Spaniards.

I really believe that our cars and medical stores, etc. were commandeered because of these happenings.

Most of us believe that they constitute an actual menace to the Unit.

SUNDAY 11TH OCTOBER

George and I reluctantly rose from our comfortable beds, washed and shaved and appeared down for breakfast about 9.30 a.m.

Several of us then had a stroll through Madrid. It is indeed a wonderful city with many marvelous buildings. There are very wide streets but their shops are somewhat different from ours. We returned at 12 o'clock and proceeded to Room 516 where a meeting was to be held. Our C.O. made it clear that every member of the Unit must be present. We waited till 1.45 p.m. and at last all appeared.

Then the Commandant dropped the bombshell. He said "The following men will return to Scotland. Harry Crawford and Ernest Porter—who wish to go home—and these five men are ordered home: Angus McClean, Walter Perfect, Jack Boyd, Robert Budge and Steve Richmond. They are ordered home for disciplinary reasons, as they are a menace to the Unit."

Phew! And then the fun started.

Budge and Richmond didn't say much but McClean and Perfect argued, pleaded, swore and in fact did everything they could to get the C.O. to keep them, but he was adamant. Down we went for lunch and there some of the men absolutely refused to leave. After lunch several of them phoned the British Embassy and did all sorts of things.

However, suppertime came and then Jack Boyd tried to throw a scare on us by saying that our C.O. had handed them over lock, stock and barrel to the military authorities. All sorts of lies were told. Then they went upstairs to their rooms for their kits as they were due to leave for Alicante by train at 11.15 p.m. Budge and Richmond came downstairs with Crawford and Porter. The British Embassy had asked he Police for an armed escort to keep them safe and these men had to go upstairs for them. All the time the two women were running around with fury at the turn of events. We walked down to the station and in a wee while they were off. They would first go to

Alicante, by destroyer to Marseilles and then by train home.

We returned to the Hotel Nacional tired and absolutely run down after the days' events.

MONDAY 12TH OCTOBER

The occupants of room 527 Hotel Nacional rose late for breakfast at 10 a.m. The others of the Unit dribbled in for their coffee and someone remarked that breakfast was a thing we got in Scotland. We did very little and could not do much except wait for orders, so nothing happened today.

TUESDAY 13TH OCTOBER

George, Hal Girvan, Tom Watters and I went over to the Dental Hospital. We remained there for quite a while and were received most graciously. After the three lads had been treated we were shown over the magnificent house with all its art treasures and received an invitation to dinner any day as long as we gave them a days' notice. Words can't describe how kind they are.

We strolled back to our hotel, looking at the shops, dodging mad traffic and admiring this wonderful city.

Madrid, a señorita who looks ready for action.
Donald mentions street fighting from 15th November.

Down in the grill room of the Nacional we got orders to proceed to Aranjuez where we would again occupy the "Banco". We got the car out and put our kits into it (i.e. No 1 store van) and away we went at 6.15 p.m. I had mentioned to Miss Jacobsen that it would be wise to phone Aranjuez in order to get a meal ready but she brushed the suggestion aside. We felt very happy getting into action again. Our first duty being to get our ambulances back.

One of the vans (No. 7) is at Burguillos and the others at Cabañas. Sing songs were in demand all along the road to Aranjuez. We arrived about one hour later and joyfully trooped into the Banco and were welcomed heartily by the three servants we had left behind. Then, we discovered that the place was occupied! Since the morning a group of militia had been billeted there. Our C.O. and Miss Jacobsen had taken it for granted that all we would have to do was enter.

Off the two of them went to get the local Commandant and after a while they returned to say that we would be billeted in private houses. In the meantime some restaurant or other had been notified that we wanted dinner and this we got at 9.30 p.m. (Lunch was at 1.30 p.m.)

George and I were billeted in the house above the Banco, and occupied by the present bank clerk. We had a lovely room and gratefully got to bed at 11.30 p.m.

Aruanjuez: On the patio of the Banco d'España. Donald is seated front left, Henry Girvan behind him, and George Burleigh is on the right.

WEDNESDAY 14TH OCTOBER

Last night we were given orders to be in the local square by 9 a.m. Consequently George and I were up by 8.30 a.m. and washed and had our coffee and roll and down by 9.15 a.m. There was no one there. Then at 9.30 a.m. Miss Jacobsen turned up. We waited and waited till 10.15 a.m. and then others turned up. George and I were fed up and I told Duncan Newbigging that he'd have to do something about this, as simple orders could either be given or obeyed properly and what would we do in an emergency? Finally the whole squad was collected including the drunk cook and off we went to Cabañas.

To get to Cabañas we went up the main road to Madrid for a bit and then cut across country till we struck the main Madrid-Toledo road and down it. At Cabañas which is about 20 kms (twelve and a half miles) from Toledo we were told that the Commandant was in Olias and he alone could sanction the return of the three ambulances.

Of course Olias is the Government front line. However we went on some 15 km. to Olias and passed some motor lorries at a level crossing. I thought it was stupid to have them there especially as the rebels are at Bargas which is almost opposite, only a few miles away. At Olias our C.O. and Miss Jacobsen went to see the Commandant.

We had a stroll over to the trenches and chatted to the soldiers as best we could and I crawled along one of their dug outs. Most of the soldiers were eating and no firing was heard. The other side were having their lunch too. This was 2 p.m. by the way and all we had had since breakfast was a bunch or two of grapes each, gathered by the wayside.

Lunch break for the soldiers at the Olias front line.

Soon after we left—knowing that just about 2 p.m. the usual shelling took place. As we approached the level crossing we also approached the shells! They were not very big ones but big enough to play havoc with twelve people in a store van. We actually passed through the smoke of one which landed at the side of the road. The motor trucks were there and the drivers and soldiers were half a mile up the road running away. We arrived at Cabañas O.K. and collected two ambulances. The other was at Mocejon and another, No.5, was at Madrid. Two lads stayed at Cabañas to wait for No.5 and the rest of us went off to collect the other. No 1 went first and then No.6 and I came last driving No.2. (They had burst the ignition lock).

It didn't take long to travel the few kilometres to Macejon but all along the road we were in full view of the rebel outposts. Arriving at the village we were asked to go to the hospital where there were some wounded. George and I went in two vans. What a sight met my gaze on entering the little hospital. A soldier lay on the operating table. His right leg was fractured below and above the knee, he had a bullet through his stomach, the forefinger of his left hand was hanging by the skin and he had a wound through his right forearm. There was only one doctor and the nurses were just girls from the village. There were four other soldiers with simple wounds in the arms and legs. The tiny place was in an uproar—no morphia, no anaesthetics.

We did what we could and administered morphia to the seriously wounded man, but before that could be done I saw the doctor amputate the finger with a small surgical knife too small for the job. George got his ambulance ready and in half an hour he was rushing the man to Madrid. I prepared my bus and left fifteen minutes later for Aranjuez hospital with four sitting cases. By this time it was getting dark. The road was horrible and I averaged ten miles per hour.

At last I arrived at Aranjuez about 8 p.m., delivered my patients to the hospital, had supper at 9. p.m. (I had coffee and a roll at 8.30 a.m., a bunch of grapes at 1 p.m. and supper at 9 p.m.). George returned a few minutes later from Madrid and both of us returned to our digs dead beat.

THURSDAY 15TH OCTOBER

Our first job today was to find No. 7. Tom Watters, George Burleigh, Miss Jacobsen and I left in an ambulance for Burguillos. We arrived there about 11.30 a.m. and just as we came to the farm house where the troops were staying No.7 made its appearance.

However, practically all the troops were at the little village of Nambroca. The Commandant there was loathe to give up the bus and while Miss Jacobsen and I were interviewing him, the No. 7 ambulance was emptied. The ambulance was used to carry a machine gun, complete with ammunition and its crew. We finally got No.7 and left for Aranjuez. On the road we were stopped by the doctor of the Aranjuez hospital who asked us to return to Burguillos with the ambulance. We receive orders right and left and don't know which to obey. We disobeyed his order and arrived at Aranjuez by 2.30 p.m. for lunch. Next we went to the hospital and proceeded to load up all the trucks with our stores and medical kit. We stopped for a rest and discussed the situation.

We have reason to believe that Miss Jacobsen was really issuing her own orders and we were trailed from place to place searching for Senor Bourgello, an old "flame" of Miss J's who always avoided her. We were the mugs.

In my opinion I think we should hand over the medical stores and return home. The Spanish Government would benefit most by that action. They have an abundance of doctors but no medical kit and the authorities are trying to split us up and hamper our work.

Some think as I do, and others don't. We received orders to proceed to Mocejon and establish our base there, so when we had packed up everything we had a cup of coffee and a bun at 7 p.m. Some of us went to a bakery and bought some cakes with our pocket money because we know that we wouldn't get anything to eat before 11 p.m.

On we went and had a long detoured journey. As we approached Mocejon, only the first van had it's full lights on and the others travelled with lights dimmed. The roads were bad and the dust was thick. Often we lost sight of the red rear lamp of the van in front and just had to switch on the lights in order to pick it up again. Once I got so sleepy that my attention relaxed and the bus landed in the ditch but I managed to get it out again.

11.20 p.m. found us in Mocejon and we found the place in turmoil with all the forces in retreat. Back we went and at 2 a.m. we landed at Illescas, about half way between Toledo and Madrid. We knocked up the hospital and gratefully got into bed there.

FRIDAY **16**TH OCTOBER

This was really a blank day. Our C.O. and Miss Jacobsen went to Madrid and other places to find out whom we had to obey and where they had to go. By night time we knew that three ambulances were to remain at Illescas and three to proceed to Aranjuez. We decided that this is what would be done although it was disobeying orders from home that we were not to be split up. I stayed at Illescas and listened in to the news from London at 11.30 p.m. and then got to bed.

This evening, Cox, our cook who has been resigning since we entered France did leave for home. The doctor here at the Illescas hospital, Doctor Juan José Escaniano, is an excellent chap and speaks some English. He was Assistant Professor of Medicine in Madrid University and escaped from Toledo with a cook who follows him wherever he goes. The cook is really adept and his coffee is just lovely.

SATURDAY **17**TH OCTOBER

A beautiful cloudless morning heralded my appearance in the hospital garden. Faintly, away south west came the sound of explosions and I just knew that a big battle was going on. I had just shaved when the telephone bell rang. "Send ambulances immediately to Cabañas."

We emptied three of them and off they went. Then I was told to follow on. I jumped into No.7 and drove down the road myself. It was indeed a wonderful morning but there was all hell further down the road. I was scared and yet I wasn't.

As I neared Cabañas I met refugees streaming up the road and soldiers too. At Cabañas the other two buses were there but one had gone further on. Fred McMahon and I went over to a field to see if we could spot where the actual fighting was going on. We had hardly decided when the drove of aeroplanes came to us. Up above were two biplanes. A soldier told us that they were government planes but shortly after came the rat-tat-tat of anti-aircraft guns. Next came a shrapnel bomb and we heard the "whing" of shrapnel whistling past us. A few wounded were brought in and some serious cases rushed to Madrid in Hal Girvan's car. How I envied him—here I was doing nothing but waiting.

Joe Boyd and I had a stroll to the other side of the village to see what we could see. Here it was barricaded up with sandbags and just outside in a semicircle were the front line. At the level crossing about two miles down the road I could see a motorised column of rebels. They were just where we were at the shelling on Wednesday. Our C.O. ordered us back to the hospital and we had just arrived when the dratted aeroplanes came over again. We scattered to the fields. Two came over and turned, peeling way from each other as they did so. No.1 dropped a few bombs near the anti-aircraft guns.

No 2 was exactly overhead, it dipped and Joe Boyd said "He's going to machine gun us". But he didn't and in any case it wouldn't have been us as he had just passed us. Of course I was lying on the ground and I turned on my back to watch it. Suddenly two specs left it and I saw the two bombs whizz through the air but they landed over the other side of the village.

Just before this raid I had been ordered home to the hospital at Illescas but I wouldn't go till the raid was over. It was because I was scared and didn't want the Spaniards see that. When it was over my C.O. ordered me home again so I returned to Illescas.

Here I found that the hospital was chock-a-block with patients who had come in from villages lying just off the roadside. I returned along the road to Juncos for petrol, picked up three wounded and six women refugees with their children and conveyed them to Illescas.

Near the front line at Cabañas

Parla: Wounded fighter being helped to the waiting ambulance.

Next my ambulance was filled with twelve patients and Bill Freebairn and I set off for Madrid. We deposited our charges and called at the British Embassy for letters. Judge our surprise on finding No. 1 van there with Miss Jacobsen and George B. Here it transpired that after we had left there was an order given to evacuate Illescas and all our trucks were busy helping to evacuate the hospital and were on the road to Madrid. We sat talking for a while and I got two letters from Mum and so I felt just O.K. About 10.30 p.m. we retired to the Hotel Loris for the night.

SUNDAY **18**TH OCTOBER
We did nothing but hang on and wait.

MONDAY **19**TH OCTOBER
We went out to our base hospital at Parla but there was nothing doing for us. The Government were preparing for a big offensive.

The dressing station under the bridge at Parla

TUESDAY **20**TH OCTOBER
The big Government offensive took place and we had a very full day. I had No.7 wagon and as luck would have it I was solo. My job was to convey wounded from Parla to Madrid and stand by at Parla. The five ambulances did a real good day's work and handled one hundred cases by the end of the day. Bill Freebairn and Miss Jacobsen returned to Scotland today.

WEDNESDAY 21ST OCTOBER

The offensive was continued and we handled eighty wounded altogether.

THURSDAY 22ND OCTOBER

There was little doing but I experienced real fear today. We went up to a little white house on the way-side which had been shelled yesterday and in the dead silence surrounding the place I became really afraid. So much so that I asked George to go back for one or two kilometres. It was just terrible waiting and waiting for what? (*Editor's note: Donald's Grandfather died this day in Scotland. Donald said that as he sat on the grass overlooking the countryside, he felt as if his Grandfather was right next to him, comforting him.*) It was just after that that I realized what a lesson I had been given in Faith and how little I really had.

FRIDAY 23RD, SATURDAY 24TH AND SUNDAY 25TH OCTOBER

There was little doing—a few wounded and some sick. In all these days when there was nothing doing our C.O. was anticipating all the time and the result was that we were all on tip-toe and had to be out early in the morning for nothing. This would have been a grand time to get some real organization—fairly regular time off, etc. established. George and I stayed all night at Getafe.

MONDAY 26TH OCTOBER

This forenoon I felt very ill and when in Madrid at 10.30 a.m. decided to go to bed. My stomach was very sore and felt just as though some sharp bits of wood were in it. In bed I got very fevered and my feet were freezing. It got better in the afternoon a bit and I managed down for supper and had some clear soup and took up a bottle of soda water. I felt much better by evening—but had been about a dozen times to the toilet. The C.O. came in at 11 p.m. and said I'd better take tomorrow off too as it was probably due to bad food or water. I slept nearly all day.

TUESDAY 27TH OCTOBER

Today I felt much better. The fever had left me but my tummy feels like a sack of water with no supporting muscle. I slept nearly all day today as well.

Donald having a trim between spasmodic shelling.

Injured man, Tom Watters and Miss Jacobsen

WEDNESDAY 28TH OCTOBER

Over a week has passed since I jotted down any notes. So here is a brief summary of the "goings on": There was little doing today at Parla. We handled a few cases and while I was in Madrid with the ambulance Parla was shelled and one landed in the hospital killing two men. Of course the hospital is not marked in any way as a hospital and we believe that they were trying for the house next door which served as military headquarters.

THURSDAY 29TH OCTOBER

There was a Government push to Torrejon today and they managed to take the Torrejon on the main road but were not successful in retaking the village on the left. As a result of the push we had a busy day and I handled forty two cases most of them being sitting cases. However we did get a very bad case where a bullet entered a man's thigh punctured his kidneys, went through both walls of his stomach and into the lung emerging at his back. That was a case for San Carlos hospital.

In the evening four of us were asked to stay at Getafe. While having supper in the Getafe hospital we had a high old time with the wee nurses. In Spain the method of drinking water (except in big towns) is to hold up a special earthenware container and let a thin stream of water shoot down the throat. There is an art in it. George had a try and managed to pour most down his shirt front. The girls were in stitches laughing at him and every now and then he would shake his trousers as though the water had gone straight down. The tears were running down my cheeks. Then a young Spaniard demonstrated how it was done but his eye caught George trying to emulate the throat action and that finished it. About half a pint went down the wrong way!

Next George got the hold of a postcard belonging to one of the girls—from her boyfriend. Then there was a scramble. She said we were "*Mucho malo, mucho pinta*" i.e. (very bad, bad rouge). So George started stroking his fore finger saying "Shame, shame, double shame everybody knows your name".

Outside Getafe Hospital: Nurses, workers and Ambulance men.

FRIDAY 30TH OCTOBER

We rose about 8 a.m. One of the medical staff who has been working with us is a little bullfighter. So this morning Hal Girvan asked him to give us a demonstration in the long dormitory. This he did and then Hal said he'd be the bull. It was very funny and ended by Hal chasing him under the bed!

There was a counter attack today at Torrejon and Parla and No.7 ambulance dealt with thirty-two cases. A terrible disaster happened at Getafe. Three big Capriani three-engined bombers circled over the town and dropped three bombs on some houses next to the road. Fortunately for me I was in Madrid when it occurred.

Eight children, six women and four men were killed and several mules. The place was in a shambles and a stream of blood marked the passage of the wounded into the hospital. When we arrived they told us to get a stretcher quickly as there was a case for Madrid—pronto, but alas he was dead.

We went on to Parla and passed the bombed houses. The mess was pretty well cleared up but the blood was still on the road and the dead mules too. At Parla we got a load and set off for Madrid. The various hospitals were visited and we returned to Parla.

What a sight met our gaze as we approached the village. No.3 ambulance burnt to a cinder and No.2 wrecked! We heard the story sitting in the twilight at the roadside.

No.3 had been standing at the side of the street near the hospital. No.2 had been half way to Torrejon along with our C.O. in No. 5. Our C.O. ordered No. 2 back to Parla as they were near some artillery. Hal Girvan "put his foot on it" and bolted for Parla. When he was almost at the village it dawned on him that the three bombers were just following him. Arriving at the hospital, he jammed on the brakes and dived for the doorway while Fred McMahon dived across the street and lay flat. This was hardly accomplished when two bombs exploded as shown (*right*):

The flame and steel from the bomb set No. 3 on fire as the petrol tank was pierced. The bits of shell passed over Fred and he emerged from the dust unscathed. About two or three yards nearer No.3

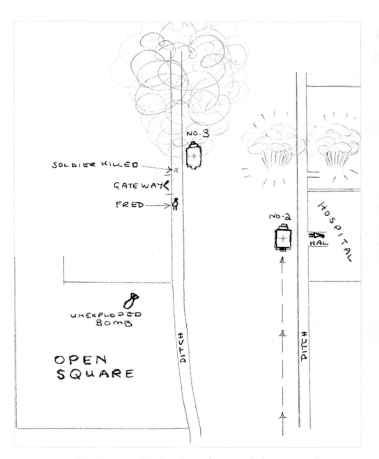

Donald's diagram of the bombing of No.3 ambulance in Parla, 30th October 1936.

Hal Girvan and Fred McMahon with their windscreen-shattered ambulance

Fred McMahon fleeing the burning No 3 ambulance at Parla

ambulance a motorcyclist was killed and a motorist was also killed. Hal was blown through the doorway into a back room. The same blast of air stripped the canvas cover from No. 2 and No.2's windscreen was perforated.

Well No.3 is now a charred wreck and No.2 was towed back to town. And that finished an eventful day.

SATURDAY 31ST OCTOBER

We should have liked to have a Hallowe'en party today but the apples are no good and treacle is un-procurable.

There was absolutely nothing doing till 3 p.m. At 3 o'clock the bl.... planes came over Getafe and we stopped just outside the town next to a culvert under the road. They bombed the trenches and the tanks outside the town (on the other side of town). Little damage was done. A little later we got a load of refugees, deposited them and went to our Hotel, to the Grill Room for dinner. It was the usual 5–7 courses of soup, fish, rice and meat, chops, sweet and fruit. There are very few people get that in Madrid today. And so to bed.

Putting out the flames

The No. 3 ambulance is burned to a cinder.

Surveying the smouldering No. 2 ambulance

November

SUNDAY 1ST NOVEMBER

Now that November has come the days and nights are getting chilly. Each morning on rising the sun streams through the window from a cloudless sky. It is lovely in the sun but the wind is chilly. At night it is distinctly cold and we have to wear our heavy overcoats. Some trees are devoid of leaves but the vast majority are gold and brown. I'm just wondering what will happen when the trees are bare and no friendly foliage obscures our ambulances from the prying eyes of airmen. As usual there was little to do at Getafe (where we are now stationed) till 3 p.m. Shortly after 3 o'clock we took two loads of sixteen men to Madrid.

One of our helpers and a good friend of us all is little Inez, our girl with the big eyes. Senorita Ines Jinumez Lumbreres was a third year medical student at Madrid University. She accompanies us and shows us the roads to the various hospitals. She is a great kid and has retreated with the doctor Juan José Escanciano (*pictured left*), from Toledo—Olias—Cabanas, Illescas, Parla and now Getafe, near Madrid. George and I took her into the hotel and she had dinner with us all. She really needed a good rest so we asked her if she would prefer to stay in the hotel overnight. Not her! So we all returned to Getafe.

George and I slept again at Getafe but it was quiet as all the nurses were now in Madrid and our hospital is now a dressing station.

MONDAY 2ND NOVEMBER

At 3.30 a.m. in the cold dark hours we were roused to take two wounded to Madrid. So out we came. One man had had his fingers amputated and the other a clean wound. We were stopped umpteen times by the guards, but of course got through O.K. One was deposited at San Carlos and the other at Republicano Hospital. Back at Getafe we got to bed and slept till 8.30 a.m. All day we dodged around and conveyed cases to Madrid but not a great deal.

TUESDAY 3RD NOVEMBER

There is no doubt about it but the organisation of the Unit is hopeless. After an "all night" duty George and I should be off duty today. As Getafe is so near Madrid (twenty minutes) four ambulances is sufficient to cater for all that comes and one ambulance should remain in Madrid. This would give us a free day in every five. If there is a "push" well we can

Dr Juan José Escanciano (left), Donald (facing right) and other ambulance men take the wounded to a dressing station just before the fall of Illescas.

always bring out the other one. But no, we get no time off and we are on duty from morning till seven and eight p.m. at night.

After dinner I am too tired and sleepy to write and just want to fall into bed. Also there has been not preventative steps taken for illnesses and for instance we have no throat gargle. We have only one sprayer for disinfecting five ambulances. I am sure that it is dangerous as it is. Our ambulance kits are not in full working order. Our C.O. should spend some time looking after this business but no he prefers being out with us. Every now and then he gets on to a dispatch riders' motorbike and careers along the road—or maybe on a horse or demonstrates the use of the bayonet, etc. In this way and by fairly frequent totes of rum he gets rid of nerves.

Another instance was that last Sunday there were two men without an ambulance yet he spent most of the day entertaining an English lady teacher in Madrid and used his ambulance for private purposes while the two men kicked their heels in the hotel.

WEDNESDAY 4TH NOVEMBER

Coming back to Madrid last night I became very cold and shivery and had a sore head and throat. Consequently I only took some hot clear soup and got to bed, taking two aspirins.

This morning I still had a temperature so decided to remain in all day. The C.O. gave me a sweating tablet which got some sweat out of me. I had a rare peaceful sleep till about 3 p.m. Then I rose and had a black coffee and until 6 p.m. wrote in this diary.

Senorita Ines Jinumez Lumbreres, third year student at Madrid University, helping the wounded with Dr. Juan José Escanciano. (See Appendix 1: Article for the Glasgow Herald.)

During the day there were many aerial alarms as the enemy planes paid frequent visits to the Capital. George came back at 7.30 p.m. and broke the news that the rebels had taken Getafe. They had cleared out the hospital and when George and co wanted to return the guards tried to stop them.

After a bit of a chat we went down for supper to the grill room and then to bed.

THURSDAY 5TH NOVEMBER

Last night I received a letter from Roy and it was like "a breath 'o fresh air frae Aberdeen." This morning my pyjama jacket was damp with sweat so I didn't go out this morning. Consequently I got two letters written—one to Mum and one to Uncle George. In my note to Mum I enclosed the two sets of snaps taken a while ago.

While at breakfast I saw an airman come down by parachute over Madrid after his plane had been shot down by another. There were various alarms as planes came over the city and they didn't know which was which. Several rounds were shot at Government planes.

After lunch I went out with George. We headed for Carabanchel suburb. It was pitiful to see streams of people men, women and children loaded up with their belongings or as much as they could carry, trekking into town. Donkeys loaded up with bedding, carts,—here and there a poor soul hugging a sewing machine. The single-decker tramcars loaded on the roof with people and bedding. We went to the suburb and soon were loaded up with refugees old and young and back we came to the city. In such a way we finished off this day.

Refugees fleeing Madrid.

FRIDAY 6TH NOVEMBER

George and I slept in this morning and it was 8.30 a.m. when we rose. Of course with the wooden "roll top" shutter in front of the window no light enters or leaves. At night when entering my bedroom I run down the shutter and then switch on the light—otherwise a bullet might fly up from the street below.

Well, after breakfast we spent the forenoon getting No.7 repaired as the inside light had failed. While doing this we saw a squadron of twelve aeroplanes circling Madrid—the Russian planes had arrived. I also had a look in one of the Russian armored cars. It was Russian alright.

A small two-inch quick-firer cannon mounted on the swivel turret and the shells were extremely long, i.e. high velocity. Also two machine guns.

(N.B. At Getafe when the Russian tanks were not acquainted with the front, at a retreat they refused to go back and let fly at everything which came round a bend on the road. In doing so one of their shells hit a Spanish tank, went through it like going through a piece of paper and also a man's leg, which was amputated at Getafe.)

After lunch we went out about a mile (the front line is two miles) from Madrid i.e. to the suburbs and waited there for wounded. While waiting I saw a great aerial battle. Five fascist planes appeared and got chased by fifteen Russian scouts. Today it was cloudy and cold and it was the cloudy sky which saved the fascists. When I returned I got a letter from Mum and got the bad news that Grandpa died a fortnight ago yesterday. Otherwise all are keeping well at home.

SATURDAY 7TH NOVEMBER

On rising today George and I wondered when we would be sleeping again in the Hotel Nacional. We have been ordered to the British Embassy to sleep and eat. Consequently as soon as we had breakfast we removed the remainder of our things to the Embassy.

In the forenoon George, Joachim (a young Spanish guide) and I went just over the Toledo bridge and stopped there deeming it unsafe to go further. George was wondering whether to turn No.7 around to face Madrid again or let it lie as it was when a shell burst just across the road. A bit of it glanced off Joachim's side as he stood outside the cab talking to me. We weren't long in turning the car round and getting to the other side and up the street a bit. Here we waited all morning and had two trips to the San José hospital. We we had lunch there then in the afternoon went over the bridge and half a mile up the Carabanchel road. One or two cases were collected there and that finished the day's work at 6.30 p.m. We had dinner in the Embassy and then went to a Britisher's house and listened-in till about 10 p.m.-returned to the Embassy and rolled into our sleeping bags.

Madrid 6th November 1936. The Russian planes have arrived.
(This photo is from a Spanish newspaper, but the Editor cannot trace the source.)

A rest for everyone between fighting.
(Editor: The location was not documented.)

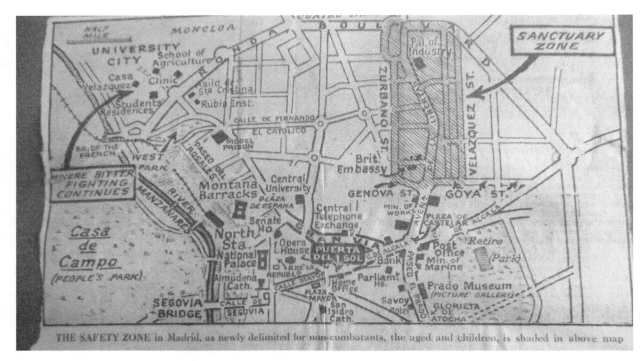

1936 Map of Madrid: See British Embassy in Sanctuary Zone. (The map of Madrid was from a newspaper but the Editor cannot trace the source.)

SUNDAY 8TH NOVEMBER

I didn't sleep too well last night on the carpet but it seems I got a better sleep than most of them. The room we sleep in is a huge rectangular one—for all the world like a room in a museum. Huge oil paintings hang on the walls, here and there old carved tables and drawers while in odd corners stand figures in medieval steel armour with swords and lances. Indeed by the light of a hurricane lamp the atmosphere is quite eerie. By the way the house belongs to the Embassy but the Embassy proper is across the road. This big house was obtained at the beginning of the war for the purpose of housing British subjects when need be.

Well we had breakfast in the Embassy of white coffee, marmalade and bread and butter (not good). Then George and I went over the Toledo bridge and stopped about a quarter of a mile up the Carabanchel road. There was absolutely nothing doing and in two hours we collected one man with a flesh wound.

Just about 11 o'clock No.1 came along and Miss Jacobsen brought us the news that the two Irishmen, Joe and Fred, had been captured. They had been told to go up the road to collect a wounded man. Their ambulance was seen to fly up the road at a terrific speed, it passed the hospital and also the guards who tried to stop them. In no mans' land the ambulance was seen to stop and one of the men left it. The fascists had beckoned them on and that is all we know.

Joe Boyd has been warned over and over about carelessness and last night one of the lads had threatened to club him if he went any further. Just after we heard the news we left for a hospital. I felt very nervous this morning and as it was Sunday decided for once to try to get a little quietness and prayer. We went to the Embassy for news and then I remained in "No.11", the Embassy annex. After lunch had some quiet time and prayer and felt much better after it.

However the quiet of the afternoon was shattered by the roar of planes and the booming of

38

bombs. The fascists were bombing part of Madrid. They had seven heavy three motor bombers and about ten scouts and they dropped a good load of bombs. Darkness came on a little later and so did suppertime and then to bed.

MONDAY 9TH NOVEMBER

Naturally we are all wondering what has happened to the two missing lads, Joe and Fred. Last night we got news that "a magnificent Scottish ambulance" had been captured—but no news of the occupants.

I didn't go out today at all. My nerves are now too active for comfort. We went over to the British-American Nursing Home and evacuated all the patients and goods to another house in the centre of the town. After this was done George made for the front but I got off at the Embassy.

It is difficult to explain what's wrong. Whenever I go near the firing line and hear the shelling my nerves begin to get control. I can feel my tummy tying itself in knots. My pipe gets into my mouth and I chew the stook. Next I try to relax but it's no good.

All my theories of Faith in God—my Faith have failed. I know full well that He is watching over me but that knowledge is of no avail. Maybe the trouble is that I am not completely surrendered to His Will. I am afraid of being split open by shrapnel. Somehow I don't mind being killed outright or having a clean wound but after seeing some of these horribly wounded men I am afraid of getting a packet like that.

Not so long ago I could claim to have "That peace which quivers like the calmest star" but that was while in the quiet and peace of home life—but now. . .Tuesday 10th November

I spent the day in clearing up the stores downstairs and also in writing a letter to Alex. We got news from the War Office that Joe and Fred were shot in the back by the rebels. Frankly we do not believe it.

WEDNESDAY 11TH NOVEMBER

Feeling much better this morning I went out with George to Puerto de Toledo. On the road there my nerves began to tell me all about it. We met Doctor Juan José, the cook and little Ines. We had a chat with them and then we went down towards the bridge. Here at the dressing station we stopped beside the other five ambulances. I told the Commandant about my nerves and he advised me to stay in the Embassy. Some of the other lads are beginning to feel nervy too.

Returning to the Embassy I was given the job of being first aid man there. There were quite a number of women children there and perhaps some shrapnel had landed between them. This evening we received definite news that Joe and Fred are safe, and are under detention by the rebels.

Donald and the admirable Spanish Interpreter
Joaquim Eusigan Morales.

THURSDAY 12TH, FRIDAY 13TH, SATURDAY 14TH AND SUNDAY 15TH NOVEMBER

There was little doing on Thursday. Hal Girvan felt ill in the evening and we took him to a hospital (at which we are well known) to be examined. There they told him that he is suffering from shock and a touch of fever and should have a rest for a week. On Friday Hal felt pretty bad and remained in bed all day. The C.O. never missed him as he was too busy entertaining others. Well this was Friday the 13th.

George was over at the Casa del Campo in the afternoon. Along came five bombers and dropped about sixty bombs round him. He said afterwards that he was shivering and praying and when George says that—well it was bad. Just when the bombers had dropped their load we saw an aerial battle. There were about thirty small scouts in the air at the same time. It certainly was a sight. In the morning there was a battle too and I saw one airman descend by parachute.

At dinner Duncan Newbigging informed us that two ambulances would leave on Saturday for Alicante with British refugees, load up with stores on Sunday and return on Monday. The big van No.1 with Tom Watters driving would go and he himself would drive in No.5.

The rest of us were astounded at the idea of the Commandant leaving us in Madrid, and going to Alicante with the possibility of being cut off. Leaving the Unit is bad enough but in such a state it is worse. The result was that we all felt sick of the whole business.

Duncan Newbigging in the Commandant's car

Saturday morning they left and there was a delay as the Commandant suddenly realised that he had no petrol in his car.

We had good news that both Joe and Fred have been released by the rebels.

This morning also a load of bombs were dropped next to the Hotel Nacional and the repercussions broke nearly all the windows in the hotel.

Hal got pretty bad and had a temperature of 103—and the C.O. went to Alicante knowing there was a sick man. However Hal picked up a bit during the day.

I set out driving No.6 with Miss Jacobsen (Katie Curran'bun) and Duncan Johnstone but it wobbled so much that we decided to take it to the garage to be repaired. I drive to the Sanidad Militar garage and on passing the site of the bombing raid felt my nerves jumping and on suddenly hearing a BANG! just about lost control of the car. We arrived at the garage, obtained a "Vale" and took it to the garage.

Returning to the Embassy Duncan Johnstone and I get into No. 2 (Hal's bus) and went to the Hotel Nacional for lunch.

After lunch I was just about to start No.2 when I spotted our friend Juan Sanchez. I yelled to Duncan and we both went forward to greet him. Then we saw him touch the black scarf round his throat. I said "José?" and he nodded. Then he told us how his brother had been shot in the chest by an explosive (dum-dum) bullet, yesterday, and died four hours later.

I couldn't speak as I felt stunned. There he was—no father, mother, sister or brother—alone.

He got in beside me and I drove him to his Asalto headquarters where his brother lay. We didn't speak on the road. José and Juan had become friends with Duncan Johnstone and myself. I had fondly thought that after the war we would write and visit each other. The two boys were so attached to each other. They were so contented together and should we find one alone he was sure to be looking for the other.

At Parla I had spent quite a time in the ruined church playing a broken organ and listening to José playing too. José was so kind and such a student. He taught himself English by reading English grammar.

The two brothers neither drank nor smoked. They always had a kind and cheery word for us and were efficient and thoroughly reliable soldiers. If the army of the Government was composed of such as these, the war would have been over long ago.

José has passed over and is now in the arms of Jesus. He is at rest and is happy. He died doing his duty.

Poor Juan. He would have liked me to go in to see José but I was too overcome. Duncan went in and on returning I could see how affected he was also.

That was 3 p.m. At 4 p.m. we attended the funeral. We put a large wreath of red flowers on the bonnet of our car. Juan looked so desolate as he followed the hearse. So alone. All the light had gone from his eyes—just staring at a black void before him. And I helpless beside him—knowing no Spanish and little French but language didn't count. He understood. José was laid to rest while the setting sun shed its wan rays on the sad company.

Time waits for no man. The night fled and Sunday came round again. Sunday—but not a day of rest. The air was filled with the roar of aeroplanes—the shuddering roar of bombs, the crack-crack of "archies" and the rat-tat-tat of machine guns.

Hal is much better physically but his nerves are like mine and both of us jump when we hear a BANG! Both of us feel that the best thing to do would be to go home. When our Commandant returns I'll tell him that I can't carry on here and I want to go home.

We can now do very little in Madrid as it is now street fighting.

If we could go to Barcelona and proceed to a front near there, again working in the country perhaps we could do more good. It would be a change for us all and much better and more sensible than waiting here in Madrid. However, we'll see.

MONDAY 16TH NOVEMBER

There wasn't very much doing during the day. We had several air raids out on the Casa del Campo and George landed right among the bombs.

In Madrid there is a scarcity of food, but the misdistribution of food has much to do with the scarcity. George has been operating near a storage warehouse and over a period of several days has been given nearly 100 dozen eggs.

On the road he'll stop when he sees some old "body" and gives her half a dozen. The Embassy has benefited from him and of course so have we.

We have been given a little room with a gas stove and there we make tea and scrambled eggs. It is like the stories of the boarding schools where the boys have feeds.

One morning we scrambled fifteen eggs (!!) I'm ashamed to say.

Hal got up this afternoon and did a bit of driving.

About 5 p.m. Juan Sanchez came along. We were terribly glad to see him. He has four days leave to go to Valencia but couldn't get hold of a car. Hal and I tried to arrange to drive him to the coast but it couldn't be done. However "Katie Curran'bun" enquired about a car and was successful.

Then Hal, George, Duncan Johnstone and myself accompanied Juan to the Hotel Nacional and we had dinner there. Juan was exceedingly pleased to be able to meet us and see us again. We exchanged addresses and promised to write each other. He told us that he hated being alone as he brooded so.

He is going to Valencia and there will see José's fiancé. We gave him some food from our stores and he said he'd eat it with the girl, telling her of the Scottish ambulance men and especially of Duncan Johnstone and Donald Gallie. After dinner we took him to the garage where he is due to leave and he got a shake down for the night.

The two inseparable brothers Juan and José Sanchez Gonzalez at Getafe.

We promised to send him some copies of the photo taken with his brother in Getafe. It is the last snap of them together. Then we said "Au Revoir".

That was about 10 p.m. Earlier in the evening Madrid experienced an air raid. About 7 p.m. a plane came over and did some night bombing. The bombs were incendiary ones and consequently the sky was filled with the ruddy glare of burning buildings.

Coming along the road I said to Hal "What's that like?" "Dixon's Blazes" he replied, and so it was. Some dropped near the Hotel Nacional and one actually on the Hotel but little damage was done to it. We went up to the "Telefónica" and had bird's eye view of the blazing buildings. It was terrible and awe inspiring—fear-inspiring.

I saw the newspaper reporters making the wires red hot with news to the whole world.

Next we had a jaunt round the fires and I tried a snap—fifteen second exposure of one of the buildings.

The reporters were so impressed that they wanted to send off late news and so we returned to the Telefónica exchange. Then back to the Embassy and made some tea about 12.30 a.m. and got to bed at 1 o'clock.

TUESDAY 17TH NOVEMBER

Little happened today and probably the only incident to note was the return of the ambulances from Alicante. Before the ambulances arrived however some of us went down to San Carlos hospital to visit an English doctor who was in one of the wards there, and to see if it would be possible to have him transferred to the British-American Nursing home. However on enquiry we found that it was not possible as he could not be considered a British subject, for some reason, and there might be political complications.

Two of the ambulances, George Burleigh at the door of No.7 and the C.O.'s car.

WEDNESDAY **18**TH NOVEMBER

The day started early. At 2.30 a.m. I was wakened by the noise of bombing and I could hear the roar of planes overhead. It was not at all pleasant especially as the bombing sounded quite near. The palace of the Duke of Alba was struck by incendiary bombs and destroyed by fire.

This forenoon Hal felt pretty bad and stayed in bed—while I spent the forenoon collecting beds and refugees and taking them to the Embassy. Then I took Hal to the British-American Nursing Home as we thought he's be much better there.

After dinner tonight we went down to our "cubby hole" and held a meeting and had a cup of tea. All or nearly all of our grievances were put forward and discussed. It was impressed on me that I am by no means a passenger and that there is much work to do—cooking etc. and I certainly should stay.

It was all agreed that we all were suffering from nerves and that as we could do little work we would all take it easy until the climax had passed. It was also agreed that instead of being issued with cigarettes we would get 10 pesetas a week as allowance—that means 17 pesetas per week in all. Whoopee!

George also presented us with 8 pesetas each which he had obtained for eggs.

I went to bed feeling ever so much happier than I have been. I had a job before me—making breakfast.

THURSDAY **19**TH NOVEMBER

Ups I get at 8 a.m. and made a bee line for our wee kitchen across the road. I got the kettle on the gas ring (I'm using our petrol camp stove) and then got out the oatmeal which we have brought from Scotland.

In a wee while the porridge was bubbling nicely on the stove. Although I say it myself it was grand and the boys just lapped it up. This was followed by fried eggs with buttered rolls and coffee. What a spread! Gosh! It was nearly lunch time when I was finished doing "orderly" work. Then I got No. 6 out of the garage and had lunch.

The afternoon was spent with Hal in the Nursing Home. While I was there fifteen mighty three-engine bombers came over and played havoc in Madrid and on the Casa del Campo.

When I saw George he pointed to old No.2. A bomb had burst behind it and a piece of shrapnel had gone right through from back to front emerging through the windscreen just at the steering column—George was "in a blow a brig" when it happened—otherwise he'd have been badly wounded.

After dinner (which we got in the dining room and was a bit scanty) we retreated to our kitchen and I made some tea and we had biscuits and cheese. Today we've been more together than we've been for a long long time. We've been together at breakfast and after dinner and all the days' happenings are related, discussed, commented on, etc.

We laughed when George told us of his hunting trip. He and Duncan Johnstone spotted a pig in the garden of the Royal Palace. So George, armed with a bayonet and a stick gave chase.

"Damn it man, that pig'll be about a hunnrd' pun' dressed," and off he set. For over an hour he chased it but never could catch it and it would stop and when he was almost on it, the pig would "give him the raspberry" and scurry away. A donkey in foal and it were friends and the pig would stand between the donkey's legs while the donkey faced up to George. However George isn't finished yet and he means to get it.

The remaining ambulance men in Aranjuez, November 1936. Donald is second left front row perched on the wheel, George is on the roof and Tom Watters is bottom right sitting on the mudguard.

FRIDAY 20TH NOVEMBER

I was up before the others this morning and when they came over I had prunes and fried eggs ready for them. It rained all day and so we were free from aeroplanes; and so passed another day in peace. In the forenoon I wrote to Dad and the afternoon was spent in a long discussion with a Moslem missionary from India.

At 5 p.m. I was due for a hot bath over in the Embassy basement so over I went. When I turned on the tap the water simply burbled out with steam. Says I to myself says I "This is too good for me alone," so I raced upstairs and spotted Tom Watters in the hall.

"What about a hot bath, Tom?"

"Sure!—ye're no kiddin'?"

"No" I replied.

So down we scampered and I got into the bath while Tom sat with only his trousers on waiting and reveling in the thought of the hot bath (it is several weeks since we had one).

Just then a knock came at the door and Tom looked out—it was one of the Spanish lassies and when she saw Tom's head and chest appearing round the doorway she let out a shriek and fled along the passage.

We simply shrieked with laughter. Then Tom scrubbed my back—Oh! it was glorious.

Next Tom had a bath and then we heard the tackity tramp of boots along the corridor. It was Duncan Johnstone.

"Whit about a bath, Duncan?"

"Sure!" and off he went for his towel.

So Duncan had a bath and then Jimmie Oldfield, a reporter came along and he had one too—complete with back scrub.

After a while we toddled up for dinner and then we heard the news that Fred and Joe had spoken over the radio to Lisbon. They said that their tyres had been punctured with bullets. Then they were marched with their hands up for 100 yards and put against a wall to be shot as the rebels thought them to be Russian. Just then a seriously wounded man was carried along and Fred administered first aid to him. The man could speak English and explained to their guards who they were.

The prisoners were brought before the Commandant who asked them military questions which they refused to answer. And so now they are waiting for a boat for Lisbon.

SATURDAY 21ST NOVEMBER

The porridge was just bubbling away nicely this morning when the Chargé D'Affaires came into the kitchen for some breakfast. He had porridge, scrambled eggs with buttered rolls and coffee and then a cigar. He declared it was the best breakfast he'd had for months.

There was little doing today and I spent the afternoon just doing odds and ends.

There are about a dozen Britishers sleeping with us in the dormitory. This evening when we came into the dormitory someone started to "meeaow" so a shoe came flying along—and then another. That was too much of a good thing. We got down flat and replied with our boots and some tin water bottles. The fight was getting quite warm when Tom Watters discovered a dozen or so oranges. Then the fight got hot and only stopped when someone knocked through from the adjacent dormitory.

SUNDAY 22 NOVEMBER

Again there was little doing today. I spent some time writing to Mum and then in the afternoon visited Hal in the nursing home and had afternoon tea with him. He is feeling much better and we chatted about all sorts of things till 7.30 p.m. While the other men in the dormitory were dining I filled their beds with peas and made apple pie beds.

The day came eventually to a close with a discussion on the merits of Ghandi.

Hal and new-found friend in the garden of the British-American Nursing Home, Madrid.
journey.

MONDAY 23RD NOVEMBER

Dull and cloudy this morning and so we didn't have any air raids today. I received a letter from Mum and also one from Robert Holley. Mum said she intends going to a Whist Drive tomorrow night with Mrs. Holley. Mrs. H. is running it for the Unit. Mr. Stott and Dad have raised £1,000 for the Unit.

The boys were very glad to hear the news and we decided to send a telegram to be read at the Whist Drive something like this:

"Best wishes to all. Our hearts are in it too." Scottish Ambulance Unit.

In the afternoon I was told to prepare No 2 wagon as we would need to go to Alicante on the coast.

So I did this, visited Hal and prepared for the

TUESDAY 24TH NOVEMBER

In the cold grey dawn at 6.30 a.m. the four vans set off with 35 British refugees. The first part of the road was misty and I wouldn't go fast at all. About 16 miles out among some low foothills I had a puncture. A bit further on we ran out of rain clouds and stopped for a rest.

It was simply grand out there in the country. Away at our rear hung the black rain clouds over Madrid, while above us they were broken with the warm sunshine playing on us below. Out came the football and we have a punt around to stretch our legs.

Then the convoy started once more and soon we drew on to the main road to Albacete and Alicante. It is a fine road and we fairly bowled along it sometimes touching 55 m.p.h. Between the villages the road is absolutely straight, the spires of the village churches being the terminal points of the straight line.

We struck Albacete about lunch time and stayed there for two hours. I spoke to a man from Glasgow who knows Tom Taylor.

About 3.30 p.m. when we were half way from Albacete to Alicante the convoy was stopped because the Commandant said he wanted half an hour's sleep!! We punted the football around till he woke again.

As we approached Alicante we zig-zagged through the mountains and it was an exciting experience in the darkness. We were all happy when we at last drew up at the door of the British Consulate at 6.30 p.m. Supper time came and immediately afterwards I slipped into bed.

WEDNESDAY 25TH NOVEMBER

The bed wasn't so good and I slept ill on it. After breakfast we went down to the quay where some seven tons of food had been unloaded from the launch of H.M.S. Woolwich. It was simply grand seeing the spick and span sailors cleaning out the boat after it had been unloaded.

There was a bit of a mix up with the stores as the Commandant wasn't there when he should have been. Eventually we stored them away in the customs house with the intention of loading the buses tomorrow morning. No 1 has a broken bolt holding the spring for the front axle and No.2 needs the tyre repaired. Tom Watters took No.1 to be repaired and we then took No.2's wheel to be repaired.

In the later afternoon George B., Duncan J., Tom W., Jermoh (Spanish guide) and myself were conducted over H.M.S. Woolwich. She didn't look grand from the outside as she is not a Man o' War but inside it was a treat for sore eyes. We bought quite a lot of 'baccy' and cigarettes from the canteen and then had a drink in the officer's mess (I had sherry).

The trip out and back in the speed boat of the destroyer "Gypsy" was worth the journey to the coast itself.

THURSDAY 26TH NOVEMBER

Yesterday was lovely and fine and just a grand day for a bathe. Today it was windy and a bit chilly but extremely mild for this time o' year. About 9.30 a.m. we went over to the Customs to load up the trucks. However we had to have a release note so I went to look for the Commandant. I found him in the hotel with Mr. Heyworth from the Embassy who had made the trip with us.

We went to the Consul for the note and there our C.O. asked Mr. Heyworth to help with the loading as he had some "personal shopping" to do.

It is worthwhile noting that he was in charge of a mission.

(1) To take British refugees to the coast. (2) To bring back supplies for the Embassy.

Well No. (1) was fulfilled but he couldn't help or supervise (2) because he had "personal shopping" to do.

Spick and span sailors loading up the vans with provisions at Alicante.

Hauling goods up onto Alicante beach.

Alicante from the speed boat "Gypsy".

Writing home from Alicante

Last night he was very definite that he would be there to check over the articles as there was a mistake made last time and if the Embassy were going to be so finicky about that he'd damn well be finicky about this. (The whole mistake was treated as a joke by everyone except him). The boys therefore loaded the trucks themselves and left a quantity of stuff for the C.O.'s wagon. After loading we went up the town to do some shopping and then had lunch.

The afternoon was simply wasted waiting to start. No one could find the C.O. and he was always absent when wanted. We waited till 5.30 p.m. before we got under way and we should have been away by 2 pm. Consequently it was 9.30 p.m. when we drew up at Albacete only to find that there was no place to sleep. However we did get some supper and it was suggested that we drive on to the next village and seek a bed there. On we went and did get beds. George and I were taken to an old sort of farm labourer's cottage.

We were shown the tiny bedroom leading from the kitchen and the owner handed us the key of the door and bid us "Good night"!

We, utter strangers, were given the use of the house. Could anyone be more trusting and kind? However that didn't finish the day. There was a little kitten in the house and did it meow! We got into bed and the little brute jumped up on the bed and meowed away—so I rose and put it into a storeroom. However it still made a racket—and I decided to put it outside. Up I got onto the cold floor again and opened the front door and put it outside, breathing a sigh of relief. I had hardly turned my back when the brute was in again via a hole at the side of the door.

In the end it spent the night in the storeroom and we dropped off to sleep about 12.30 a.m.

FRIDAY 27TH NOVEMBER

Punctually at 5.30 a.m. George and I rose, dressed and joined the others where the trucks were standing. We were on the road by 6.15 a.m. and made good progress. About 9 a.m. we stopped at a little hospital and had breakfast and a sheep was brought and tied inside a van. When we were about 20-40 miles from Madrid No. 5 had a puncture. Otherwise the journey was uneventful.

We arrived in town about 2 p.m. We were told that we wouldn't need to unload the vans as that would be done for us so after lunch we had an hours' nap and rose feeling very much refreshed.

There were two letters for me—from Karin and from Juan. I was very happy to receive both but disappointed that no word had come from home.

SATURDAY 28TH AND SUNDAY 29TH NOVEMBER

There was really very little done during these two days. I cleaned and washed out the petrol stove as it was in a filthy state and also paired off with Tom Watters for a while as he was repairing No. 5 car.

MONDAY 30TH NOVEMBER

Tom was up first this morning and consequently it was I who got the "doing". Whoever is up first usually gets the others up by jumping on them or pulling off blankets and sleeping bags.

Often we have a great set too and it is great fun. Sandy McLellan who sleeps downstairs with the C.O. in a private room does envy us up here.

The chief topic of our talks just now is Duncan Newbigging. We believe he is involved in a bigger game than the running of our Unit. He purchased many stores at Alicante and we believe he is making a big profit by selling them in Madrid—some reckon his profit on the trip at between 2,000 and 3,000 pts.

Some of us are concerned about the matter as we may be embroiled in the business as members of the Unit.

A while ago he got a prisoner released from goal and said that the Scottish Ambulance Unit would stand surety for him. That of course is utter nonsense as we know nothing of the man and it was entirely a private affair of his.

Donald in his ambulance

December 1936

TUESDAY 1ST DECEMBER

There was little doing today for us—some bombing and some shelling. In the afternoon I went over to Miss Gifford's to attend the funeral of her mother but the hearse left half an hour early in order to have the ceremony through before darkness. Duncan Johnston and I have made friends with Dick Ray-Page and Miss Gifford who live in part of the Commercial Secretariat and it is quite a relief to go there and relax into comfy armchairs in a nice clean and modern flat.

WEDNESDAY 2ND DECEMBER

I have been hoping and hoping to get a letter from home but so far no word has come.

This morning after brekker we had ourselves photographed and then Tom Watters and I took the rear wheels from No.6 and replaced them with new ones. Then we had a look at the batteries, plugs and adjusted the brakes. This job was finished by midday and Tom proposed going down to the North Station to get No.7 from George and give him No.6. I demurred a bit as we didn't know the front but went. We arrived at Estacion Norte but George wasn't there. Then we went to the Casa de Campo to look for him but didn't find him there either. I found my nerves just trying to run riot and I was relieved when we were once again in the Embassy.

At lunch I heard that a mail bag was due to leave tonight so I wrote a letter to Mum. While writing I was called to the courtyard to speak to a man and while there I heard a mighty screech overhead, then a shell bust. We dived for the doorway and were just recovering from our astonishment when another came over. Both landed in the building next door and directly opposite the Embassy. The street was full of dust and smoke and the ground strewn with broken glass. A man with his head covered in blood was brought downstairs. He jumped into an ambulance and we rushed him to hospital but it was too late. He was dead on arrival.

On returning I went in to see if Miss Gifford was O.K. and was relieved to find her so. George, Duncan J. and I had dinner there at 8.30 p.m.

THURSDAY 3RD DECEMBER

The day started as usual and the boys had their porridge and eggs. After I had cleared up I started writing a letter in Spanish to Juan and finished it in English.

Then at 1 p.m. I decided to try my hand at rice pudding with raisins. The rice was just starting to boil when Tom came in to say I was needed on a wee job—i.e. to take No.7 to a garage, etc. So perforce the gas was turned off and the rice left. Returning in an hour I found it a solid lump. However by some judicious extraction etc. the rice was cooked.

Tom and I had our lunch upstairs—a plate of potatoes and some stinking bacalao, the whole dish smelling of an unsanitary public lavatory. We were glad to run downstairs for our pudding.

After lunch we attended to No.7 again and about 4 p.m. I got Dick Page to translate all of Juan's letter into Spanish. George and Duncan J. arrived with logs for the fire and we had a cup of tea. There was a slight Government advance today. Crossing over to the Embassy we noticed many milicianos and police round the Finnish Legation. Later they broke into it and found many fascists there.

Tom and I got a loan of a short-wave radio and it was just grand listening to Ambrose and his band and also to the 11.30 p.m. news bulletin. We received the startling news of the British King's probable abdication.

I was terribly bucked to receive a letter from Mum today to say that she is feeling fine, all is well at home, and also the safe arrival of the snaps. I also received a nice letter from Edna and Roy.

FRIDAY 4TH DECEMBER

Nothing startling happened today regarding the Unit. We did get a thrill however when no less than thirty mighty three-engined bombers flew over the city, fortunately they didn't carry high explosive bombs. They dropped incendiaries near the Casa del Campo and several landed very near to George and Duncan.

In the afternoon I had a walk through the town with Dick Page and enjoyed it ever so much as I haven't stretched my legs for quite a time. George, Duncan and I had supper in No.23 (Miss Gifford's flat) and enjoyed it ever so much.

Returning to the Embassy I found the boys having a sing-song so we joined in—what a racket! All available saucepans and combs were utilized. Hoarseness made us retire at midnight.

SATURDAY 5TH DECEMBER

The morning passed uneventfully under a blue cloudless sky. There is no doubt that this is a wonderful country for climate. Every day we rise to be greeted by King Sol beaming from his blue blue heavens. If we were out in the country we could sunbathe.

Well anyway it looked as though it would be an uneventful day but at 3.15 p.m. just as Hal (now out of hospital) and I were about to set out on a shopping expedition, Allwark, the Reuter's correspondent, came to ask us to take a woman to hospital—a maternity case and her child was dead.

We did take her to hospital and there the doctor informed us that the child is alive and she would give birth in two hours. So we returned feeling that a good job had been accomplished.

Hal and I then had tea at Mr. Hall's house. We listened to the Empire News at 6 p.m., the West Regional news at 7 p.m. and to finish up I played some Scottish tunes on the piano.

After dinner we held a meeting regarding the neutrality of the Unit. Some of us just won't work for the other side unless to save our lives. Also relating to official reports going home as some of our folks are getting disquieting news.

The meeting cleared up the atmosphere a bit but we must await the report of our C.O. who is to see the Sanidad Militar. There he is to ask if they would benefit more by us moving to another front or remaining in Madrid. And so to bed.

SUNDAY 6TH DECEMBER

No one was out at the front today so George and Duncan decided that they should have a day off to write some letters. As usual it was bright and sunny. We had a ground view of an aerial dog fight but the planes were so high that we didn't get such a thrill.

I received a wonderful present of three volumes of Hutle's Engineering Manual in Spanish. They are beautiful books and the donor is Rafael, the personal body guard to the Chargé D'Affaires.

Impromptu cartoon by the Spanish poet and artist Rafael Alberti for Donald: "a Donald con todo afecto. Rafael."

Today is Mr. Ogilvie-Forbes birthday and so in the afternoon we entertained him to tea with some of his staff—we were about 20 in all. He was very pleased with the little "do" as he hadn't had a birthday treat since he left school. We listened to some of Harry Gordon's records, piping and Scottish marches. The tea party broke up at 7.30 p.m. and the S.A.U. went into their cubby hole to hear the report of our C.O.'s visit to the Sanidad Militar.

He produced a written statement that the Sanidad is very well pleased with us indeed and are most grateful for our services. They are going to provide us with a house, lay a telephone into it and we shall take turns sleeping there.

From the C.O.'s report I felt that it is doubtful if he presented the case as the boys wished. They definitely want to go out into another sector away from Madrid but if the Sanidad specifically want them here they will remain. We don't know yet if the authorities do want us here indefinitely. Although I deemed it a poor report and believe that several times he "hedged" the major issue. However that is my personal opinion.

After the meeting George, Duncan J. and I had a very nice supper with "Mischief" and Dick Page.

Miss Gifford (Mischief) is returning to London and feels very pessimistic about it but cheered up considerably on learning that we will probably run her down to Alicante. I had a little drink of her home-made liqueur—"Cointreu". Miss Gifford gave me the recipe:

COINTREU
Ingredients:
Half litre Alcohol (95% Abs.)
1 Orange
Half litre water
400 grams sugar

In a hermetically sealed jar suspend an orange 1" above half a litre of Alcohol (Abs.) for 3 weeks. The orange "sweats" and the beads of "sweat" fall into the alcohol.

Take half a litre water and add 400 grams sugar. Boil for 5 minutes and then add the alcohol (+ orange sweat). Filter Several Times. When cold bottle and drink carefully.

We toddled back to our mattresses about 11 p.m. and as usual at night we could hear plainly the shelling, machine gunning and rifle firing.

MONDAY 7TH DECEMBER

The most important happening today was the arrival of 3 letters—from Emma, Alex and Aileen. It was fine hearing from them again and Alex included a snap taken in Glasgow of Betty and myself.

As usual at breakfast before our C.O. came in and after Miss Jacobsen had left there were various discussions about the Unit all showing discontent with the organisation and showing how fed up we all are.

In the afternoon (after eating a lunch I had made—chips, bully & peas followed by rice & raisins with pineapple & a cup of tea or cocoa) I sallied forth and bought three gramophone records to send home. One of them was "La Paloma Bianca". However, as I was buying them I was thinking that I'd probably take them home myself.

And so passed today.

TUESDAY 8TH DECEMBER

The first thing I did this morning was to write up the following on the writing pad used as a notice board:

To Mr. D. Newbigging.

Please accept my resignation as a member of the Unit and would you kindly arrange for me travelling to Glasgow.

Reason for returning home: When working at the front my nerves take control. Consequently, I am unable to work and will not be a passenger in the Unit.

Donald Gallie

8-12-36

Alicante—Donald's and his compatriot's luggage being loaded onto the Launch of HMS Greyhound for the journey home.

Going Home—Alicante to Marseilles—Sailors on the British destroyer HMS Greyhound. The end of an adventure.

Biography

Donald Gallie was born on 6th October 1911 in Gartsherrie, near Coatbridge, Scotland. When he and his family moved to Lenzie, Donald attended Bellahouston Academy, played rugby for the Lenzie rugby team, became an accomplished piano player, loved opera and the Glasgow Orpheus Choir; his father was the Secretary to the Choir for a time.

Donald graduated from Strathclyde University as a Chartered Mechanical Engineer, he went on to get a Teacher's Training Diploma at Jordanhill College and a Certificate in Management Economics. While at University Donald served on the Student's Representative Council and was also active in the Student Christian Movement, attending and organizing meetings and conferences with other Universities.

As this was the height of the Depression and jobs were almost unprocurable, Donald offered to work without wages during the summer of 1936 at the local garage at Kirkintilloch so that he could get practical experience in vehicle mechanics and repair. This inspired him to volunteer for the Ambulance Unit.

Donald's father was very supportive of his son and he and his wife, Margaret, helped to raise money for the Unit. Charles Neill Gallie was Secretary General of the Railway Clerk's Association, twice President of the Scottish Trades Union Council and a Director of Cable and Wireless.

Donald's love of travel started at an early age and all his working life he travelled the globe with Karin, his Swedish wife who he married in 1938. Donald became manager of the WD & HO Wills No.4 factory in Bristol after he, backed up by the Research and Development team, invented new machinery to produce more moist tobacco by using an early form of microwave. (The company made Players and other cigarettes.) The new machinery was sold worldwide. His achievements did not go unnoticed and he was offered a post first with AMF (American Machine and Foundry) and later with the Lorillard Limited in Geneva where he lived for twenty years, becoming Co-Managing Director. He had a stint as head of the company's Far East section in Hong Kong where he and his American based company introduced Kent cigarettes to the Far East. Donald returned to Europe where he headed the European section from Brussels. Donald never forgot his Scottish roots and after his retirement visited his sister Betty in Lenzie and his brother Roy in Edinburgh regularly. Donald and Karin had four children; two dying young, leaving Michael, now in the U.S.A., and Nina in England who has transcribed and edited his Diary.

Post script: At one time whilst working in Hong Kong Donald flew to the Philippines to see for himself why cigarette production had stopped in one of his company's factories there.

On arrival at the factory not only did Donald instantly ascertain the problem but told the engineers how to get the machinery working again. Astounded, the factory manager asked Donald how he knew what was wrong.

"Well," Donald quite simply replied, "I invented it."

Editor.

Appendix 1

Three articles for the Glasgow Herald.

ARTICLE 1

28th October 1936

TO MADRID BY AIR

Miss Jacobsen will fly from Croydon to Paris today, and she will also travel by aeroplane from Toulouse to Madrid.

Interviewed yesterday by a representative of "The Glasgow Herald," Miss Jacobsen explained that when she left the unit last week it was operating at Parla, a small town in the Illescas area, which is on the direct line of the rebels' advance on Madrid. During the past few weeks it has been working in many parts of the Toledo front.

Its personnel now numbers 10, including Mr Duncan Newbigging, a Glasgow student in the final year of his medical course, who is in command, and Miss Jacobsen. The others are Thomas Watters, Torrisdale Street, Glasgow; Duncan Johnstone, Southcroft Street, Glasgow; Stewart Girvan, Hertford Avenue, Glasgow; George Burleigh, Kilsyth; Donald Gallie, Lenzie; Joe Boyd and Fred McMahon, Belfast; and Alexander M'Lellan, Ballantrae.

In the interview Miss Jacobsen spoke with enthusiasm of the courage and the energy with which the men applied themselves to their humanitarian work. She pointed out that on many occasions the members of the unit had to go right into the firing line to get the wounded.

AMBULANCES BOMBED

"They are doing splendid work, and have taken a tremendous number of wounded and soldiers ill with enteric fever to hospital. The ambulances have often been bombed, but this has not deterred our men from their work. They have displayed remarkable coolness.

One day Thomas Watters drove an ambulance along a road on which shells were busting. He is a Corporation bus driver, and he drove that ambulance with as little concern for danger as he would drive a bus through Knightswood.

"On the morning that Olias and Cabanas fell we had a gruelling time. Alexander M'Lellan went out that day and packed 16 wounded men into his ambulance. "There was no room for himself inside, so he clung on to the canvas covering behind. The route taken by the ambulance was bombed all the time by aeroplanes and was under machine-gun and rifle fire."

These, said Miss Jacobsen, were only two of many instances of the courage of the men in the unit. The Spanish people were very grateful for the work of the Scottish Ambulance team.

ARTICLE 2

Report dated 13th November for the Glasgow Herald by J.R. Allwark, Reuters correspondent in Madrid.

MADRID, FRIDAY

The proximity of the enemy to Madrid was brought home to the inhabitants of the capital today with a vengeance when, within the space of five hours, there were four air raids.

The first was at half-past eight in the morning, when the sirens screamed, and anti-aircraft guns and any other firearms available were let off in the hope of bringing down one or more of the insurgent 'planes.

It would appear, however, that the first raid was the reconnaissance type, as no bombs were dropped. At 10 o'clock the 'planes came back, and this time dropped bombs on the Casa del Campo.

I personally watched an air raid on one of the outlying districts of Madrid as I was coming back from the Illescas front line this morning. I had gone down to the front with one of the Scottish ambulance unit, who are working like Trojans in this sector.

PART OF ROAD BLOWN UP

Returning along the main Toledo road, which had been blown up in parts to prevent the insurgent advance, we were held up as usual at the cross-roads for our papers to be examined.

Just at that moment we heard the sound of aeroplane engines, and perceived three huge three-engined machines painted black. They were flying slowly and very majestically, and were escorted by four small fighters.

I left the car hidden as best I could under some trees at the side of the road and watched the planes' progress.

The work of the Scottish ambulance unit on the Illescas front is meeting with praise on all sides, and one of the doctors on that front told me today that in the past week he had brought in 800 wounded men and over 1200 refugees from the villages in or near the firing line.

ARTICLE 3

Donald Gallie, New Year 1937 (*Edited by Nina Stevens*)
WITH THE SCOTTISH AMBULANCE UNIT IN SPAIN

The outstanding feeling we (*the members of the Ambulance Unit; Ed.*) had on leaving the shores of Spain was one of unstinted admiration for the courageous struggle and magnificent determination of the youth of Spain to secure their ideals and maintain their faith in Democracy. It would take volumes to describe individual incidents and heroic personalities. But outstanding amongst these, with whom it was my privilege to work, were Dr. Juan Jose Escanciano and Senorita Ines Jinumez Lumbreres (known to us all as "little Ines"). Before the revolution Dr. Juan Jose was assistant professor of medicine in Madrid University. He is an outstanding personality, indefatigable; rest periods were quite a secondary consideration for him. Our arrival for service at Illescas, at two o'clock in the morning, was quite unexpected, and in less than half an hour he had beds available for the Ambulancia Escocesa. Dr Juan Jose had a fundamental belief in democracy for which no sacrifice was too great.

Helping him were assistants, men and women, slaving from early morning till well into the night, occasionally snatching an evening off for leave. His male assistants took their turns at night duty and were prototypes of their beloved medico. The nurses—young untrained girls—unobtrusively and efficiently vied in the efforts to keep a cheery atmosphere in a situation tense with pain and suffering.

In the lull of explosions an ambulance is heard arriving at the station. Men and girls run out and soon in perfect order the slow procession wends its way into the hospital; some wounded learn on the shoulders of girls and men—with stretcher cases in the van. Murmuring words of comfort to the bleeding victims, the girls "mother" the wounded while first-aid work is carried out. Foremost amongst these unsung heroines was little Ines, always there when wanted—scissors, peroxide, bandages—these necessaries appeared almost automatically. When night arrived, she would be so tired that it was almost too much of an effort to get to bed—but never so tired that she failed to give us a wan smile and shaking her finger at one of us would exclaim, "Mucha Pinta" (big rogue). In livelier moments, her good night was a verse of the "Internationale." Little Ines of the big heart and full of courage will always be remembered. She was a third-year medical student in Madrid University and joined the Unit by retreating with us from Illescas to Madrid.

During the whole of our sojourn in Spain we were treated with the greatest cordiality, and frequent reports of our activities and the comradeship which existed between us and the Miliciano appeared in the Madrid newspapers. Generous hospitality was always available.

Appendix 2

Donald's overview of the situation in Spain and his summing up.

After the War Donald summed up the essence of the months in Spain as follows:

"The drive to Spain was relatively uneventful except for a few of the team would drink too much. We were billeted in a house in Aranjuez, a town seven miles west of Madrid. Franco's forces were located about forty miles west of Madrid and advancing fast. We shuttled between the fighting area and the nearest First Aid post, and between this post in the village of Parla to a hospital in Madrid. Eventually the government forces were pushed back to the outskirts of the Capital. Franco's forces then began to circle the town.

There was still a British Embassy there, where we were billeted. Actually there was no further need for us there as there was plenty of vehicles and drivers to ferry casualties to the hospitals. An agreement between Franco and some foreign governments was made whereby the area in which their embassies were located would not be bombed.

This agreement was breached and bombs started to fall. There were quite a number of ex-patriots sheltering in the British Embassy. We were requested to drive them to Alicante on the coast. Arrangements had been made with the Royal Navy to ferry them to Marseilles. Some of us decided that we had come to the end of our usefulness and requested to be returned to Britain with the last of the ex-pats.

The little pocket money we were given allowed me to buy film for my camera so I have quite a good album of photographs. We got a 'lift' on a British destroyer (the HMS Greyhound) to Marseilles. We then travelled overland to Calais, across the Channel to Dover, on to London, and so to Scotland. There was no phone in our house so my arrival home came as a complete surprise. Naturally my mother was very relieved to see me."

Appendix 3

Donald's appraisal of some of the members of the Unit as of 7th October 1936.

JOHN BOYD (known as Jack). Age about 28-30. Transport Officer.
Reason for Volunteering: Not known. John is bumptious, has a superiority complex, very unreliable, too patriotic to be sincere. He was instrumental in organizing the transport. He did most of it himself and made several bad mistakes such as the design of the ambulances. Flares up at trivial things and has Hun officer complex.

ROBERT BUDGE. Age 27. Driver.
Reason for Volunteering: Partly humanitarian. He is very serious in his outlook. Is genuine but tends to be aggressive. Has not had a great education and does not pretend to be educated. One great fault is his drinking habit.

GEORGE BURLEIGH. Age 35. Driver and Ambulance man.
Reason for Volunteering: Partly humanitarian. He is one of the best. Does not claim to be a great thinker but always thinks before expressing opinion. He had had great experience in ambulance work especially as a leader of the Mine Owner's Rescue Brigade at Coatbridge. He has simple wants and enjoyments. Keen on sport and played for Rob Roy. He is a most lovable chap and one who can be relied on in precarious moments to give both sound action and advice. Of bulldog breed.

WILLIAM COX. Age ? Cook.
Reason for Volunteering: Adventure and change of conditions. He is out cook and is a regular tough guy. Has travelled the world over in the navy and mercantile marine. His chief fault is drink. He is very direct and honest and creates many a laugh. His cooking is not up to much but as a member of the Unit he is of great value. Since coming to Spain he says that his two arms are sore from trying to speak the lingo. He swears like a trooper/sailor and navy mixture.

WILLIAM FREEBAIRN. Age ?
Reason for Volunteering: Medical experience and partly humanitarian. He is a genuine chap, inclined to be highly strung. This trait leads him to make decisions lacking thought and consideration. He is Tory in outlook and thinks a lot of the British uniform.

HARRY GIRVAN (known as Hal). Age 26. Driver and Ambulance man.
Reason for Volunteering: Fed up with home conditions. Hal is also a genuine chap with a chunk of fun running through his nature. He is up to all the fun and tricks that are going. Can be relied on in a pinch. A rough diamond.

MISS FERNANDA JACOBSEN (Nickname Katie Curran' Bun) Age ? Liaison Officer and Interpreter.
Reason for Volunteering ? Miss Jacobsen is highly strung, fairly headstrong and a hard worker. She is unable to comprehend and visualize most of the situation externally and internally. Would like to have her hand in everything.

DUNCAN JOHNSTONE Age 21. Medical.

Reason for Volunteering: For medical experience. Duncan is the youngest in the Unit but is old in his thoughts and actions. He is wrapped up in his profession and studies. He is a genuine chap and a thorough student. Pleasant to speak to and willing to listen.

ALEX MCLENNAN (known as Sandy.) Age about 30.

Reason for Volunteering: Partly humanitarian and partly adventure. Sandy is a good sound lad. Intemperate regarding wine but that is his only fault. Rough and ready but polite and true. Game for anything. Can be relied on in a pinch.

FRED MCMAHON Age 24. Driver.

Reason for Volunteering: Humanitarian via politics. Fred is one of the best. Politics covers most of his horizon, ready at all times for a bout in discussion. Can be relied on in a pinch. Has a great sense of humour, is an inveterate gambler but takes his losses smiling.

DUNCAN NEWBIGGING Age 27. C.O. Medical

Reason for Volunteering: Medical Experience. Curious personality. As a man he is very pleasant, owns up to mistakes and readily apologizes for them. As a commandant he is of no use whatever. He lacks the essentials of a C.O. and just lets the Unit drift. He lacks initiative and proper respect for the men's health and interests. He is early swayed and loves to be in the "front page" of all experiences. The command of the Unit is going to his head.

ANGUS MCCLEAN Age about 27.

Reason for Volunteering: Women, wine and adventure. He's highly sexed, a drunkard, has a superiority complex, shallow, easily annoyed. Appears to have had his own way at home. Handsome and well built, he is forever after women and has spent most of his nights since leaving Britain in brothels or with women.

Appendix 4

A letter from Donald to his girlfriend Karin in Sweden.

Ambulancia Escocesa
Embajada Britanico
MADRID
27th October 1936

My Dear Karin,

I am wondering what you are doing now. How are you keeping? How are you getting on with the kiddies and are you liking the children's hospital? Your letter reached me a week or two ago (about 9th Oct.) and I cannot remember whether I replied to it or not. I have very little spare time and when I do have time to write, I send off a letter home to keep my little mother from worrying.

Yesterday I was ill with pains in the stomach and remained in bed all day and today I am feeling much better but am remaining in my bedroom. The doctor says that probably I have got infested by some bad water. Outside of Madrid one must be very careful as the water is not too good.

We have been doing quite good work lately and for the three and a half weeks that we have been in Spain we have dealt with about 1,000 wounded—many not serious but others very serious, and so we have been able to save lives and alleviate suffering. Sometimes we have only a few cases for several days and then get maybe 100 all in one day. Our base is now Madrid.

We have rooms in this luxurious hotel and we return here each night to sleep and then go out in the morning—however two men and an ambulance remain at the dressing station each night for emergencies. Of course we take it turn-about. I have seen dead and dying, seriously wounded and clean wounds and most of the horrors. Thank God there has not been any gas.

In my kitbag I have two souvenirs—a piece of shrapnel and a piece of high explosive shell picked up where we were shelled and bombed.

We are working on the main road from Madrid to Toledo—about 20 km from Madrid. In fact the ambulance only takes about 30 minutes to go from Madrid to the front line! Our dressing station has been in Parla for the last week or so but now it is in Getafe. Enclosed is a photo (not a very good one) taken by a press photographer at Cabanas on 17th October—an hour later the rebels were in the village and that night they were in Illescas—while the two nights previous I had slept at Illescas. Just after the photo was taken we heard the drone of three aeroplanes and we scattered to the fields while the anti-aircraft guns went phut-phut-phut into the blue sky—then came the BOOM! of a bomb from one aeroplane. Right about me was another. I saw it drop and just after it had passed over me two big "pills" left it—then BOOM! BOOM!

Sometimes even with fear in one's heart one has just to pray hard and get on with the work. Just before these aeroplanes came over my Commandant ordered me to go back to Illescas but when I saw the planes come over I said "I'll be damned if I'll leave till the bombing is over—the Spaniards won't call me a coward." So I waited until the raid was over and then left for Illescas.

When Madrid is in danger (and that might soon be) we shall go to the British Embassy and work there until the danger is over. We still don't know when we'll be home—maybe this side of Xmas and maybe in January or later. We are having lovely weather—blue sky all day and warm sunshine, while at night it is chilly and the sky bright with stars.

We left Glasgow with 19 men and 1 woman interpreter. Now there are only 9 men! Some wanted to go home as they had had enough and some were sent home for "disciplinary reasons" (chiefly drunkenness and immorality). When drunk they were a perfect menace to the Unit. In Spain no-one gets drunk and it is almost a crime to get drunk, yet in Spain they make tons and tons of wine. The interpreter was recalled as her work was finished. So now we are 9.

I think that is all the news meanwhile Karin dear. You might have to pay postage on this letter as I am hoping to send it by King's Messenger from the British Embassy—it will then be carried to London and posted to you from there. That is the safest way.

Are you coming to Lenzie at Xmas? If you are, then I do hope that this war will be over by then.

Cheerio meanwhile dear one and God bless you and keep you always.

Love

Don

Editor's note: This letter has been included because the original is now over seventy years old, fading and becoming brown. It will not be with us forever, and it seems a shame not to include Donald's feelings—not just the events written down in his Diary, and the overview is valuable too.

Map showing the key positions of the Ambulance men in between Madrid and Toledo September-December 1936

BETTER TO DIE ON YOUR FEET THAN · Dolores Ibarruri · (La Pasionaria)
· LIVE FOR EVER ON YOUR KNEES ·